THE ART AND DISCIPLINE OF STRATEGIC LEADERSHIP

MIKE FREEDMAN

with Benjamin B. Tregoe

McGraw-Hill

New York Chicago San Francisco Lisbon London
Madrid Mexico City Milan New Delhi
San Juan Seoul Singapore
Sydney Toronto

The *McGraw·Hill* Companies

3 4 5 6 7 8 9 0   AGM/AGM   0 9 8 7 6 5 4 3   (HC)

1 2 3 4 5 6 7 8 9 0   DOC/DOC   0 9 8 7 6 5 4   (PBK)

ISBN 0-07-141066-X   (HC)

ISBN 0-07-144121-2   (PBK)

This publication is designed to provide accurate and authoritative information in regard to the subject matter covered. It is sold with the understanding that the publisher is not engaged in rendering legal, accounting, or other professional service. If legal advice or other expert assistance is required, the services of a competent professional person should be sought.

—From a declaration of principles jointly adopted by a committee of the American Bar Association and a committee of publishers.

 This book is printed on recycled, acid-free paper containing a minimum of 50% recycled, de-inked fiber.

To my wife, Avril,
and our children—"my Caroline,"
Gemma, David, "your Caroline," and Anna.

Contents

Preface

In the 15 months since this book was first published, our volatile world continues to change at an ever increasing pace and each new day increases the key imperative faced by all organizations: that without strong strategic leadership the risk of failure increases dramatically.

During this time we have had a war in Iraq, which has seen more soldiers killed since peace was declared than during the actual war. The strategic intelligence basis for the war has been found badly wanting. SARS threw Southeast Asia and China into a tailspin and Canada into outright panic. Bird influenza is doing the same. More such previously unknown virus-related diseases are predicted. A global pandemic is feared. Those infected by HIV/Aids increase exponentially. In the meantime, dramatic advances by scientists have shown we can clone humans and get to Mars. Obesity is now the number one health concern in the United States.

The U.S. dollar is at a 12-year trough against sterling and at an all-time low against the Euro. Only Japanese Central Bank interventions to the tune of $100 billion have prevented the dollar from crashing to an all-time low versus the yen. Interest rates in the United States and Japan can hardly get lower, yet growth has been sluggish and unemployment is rising.

In global boardrooms, greed, poor governance, and incompetent management plague far too many FTSE 100 and Fortune 500 companies and their equivalents around the world. Take three examples: the proposed compensation package for Jean-Paul Garnier, the CEO of GlaxoSmithKline (GSK), the world's second largest pharmaceutical firm, was thrown out by a revolt of the majority shareholders, much to the embarrassment of Sir Christopher Hogg, GSK's Chairman.

Conrad Black is alleged to have shared $300 million in unauthorized payments to himself and his cronies. Hollinger Inc. is now engaged in a battle for the control of its major assets, its newspaper titles, including the *Daily* and *Sunday Telegraph* in the United Kingdom, the *Jerusalem Post* and the *Chicago Sun Times*. Black was ousted as CEO, yet retains voting control. Lastly, the Italian food giant, Parmalat, owned by the Tanzi family, many of whom are now in jail, was found to have a 10 billion Euro black hole in its accounts. It had been there for years! Shareholders, management, auditors, the tax authorities must have known about it or been unbelievably ignorant and incompetent.

In the United States and United Kingdom, government and regulators are looking at ways of preventing the culture of "payment for failure" as executives continue to pay themselves huge exit "bonuses.". Michael Eisner has just been ousted as chairman at Disney by a shareholder revolt disgusted no doubt by his $1 billion compensation during his relatively short tenure. A multimillionairess, Martha Stewart, an icon of "wholesome" American values, felt compelled to earn a few dollars more by insider trading, greed personified!

Sir Phillip Watts, the chairman of Shell, has just resigned after weeks of resistance following his admission that the company has 20 percent less oil reserves than had been declared years ago, when he was responsible for exploration and production and therefore for such forecasts. His announcement and subsequent intransigence wiped untold millions off Shell's and other oil companies' share prices overnight. Now U.S. regulators fear that where there is smoke there is fire.

The offer of the chairmanship of Sainsbury's, the United Kingdom's third largest food retailer, to Sir Ian Prosser was withdrawn when institutional shareholders made it known that, on the basis of his poor performance at Bass/Six Continents, he was not the man for the job.

The European Union now has another 10 members, mostly from the east, to shelter and nurture under its umbrella. China is the world's number two economic power, rapidly catching up to the United States. It is now the largest mobile phone market in the world and the second largest market for automobiles. Its GDP growth continues at 8 percent annually.

European prime ministers fight to stay out of court on corruption charges, the president of Georgia is removed in a bloodless coup, Colonel Ghadafi in Lybia is now everyone's friend, and a thriving black market in nuclear weapons components has been uncovered.

In the face of the recent pension and benefits scandal, 77 million baby boomers in the United States are due to begin to retire in 2008 and slightly fewer are due to do so in Europe. This grey power will change consumption patterns whether or not their state and private pensions are diminished.

The peaks and troughs of global activity rise and fall to even greater heights and depths than ever before. And these movements are close together in time. This "volatility quotient" continues its instability at an increasing pace.

These events are only the tip of the iceberg of the last 15 months. Is it any wonder that strategic leadership is at a premium?

The key message in the hardback edition of this book is that without a strong leadership team in place and a clear strategy process that enables them to set, implement, and update its strategy, no organization can hope to succeed in today's hostile world. That message continues to resonate even more today as effective leaders are in ever short supply.

Those who continue to question the relevance of a top team's focus on the strategy process and the value of a clear strategic vision amid such volatility, and who argue for daily operational excellence or the maximization of financial returns, need to explain how a directionless ship led by a captain with no map or compass would ever get anywhere!

I trust that those who read this book will gain some insights on how to create and maintain the strategic leadership necessary to keep their organizations on the leading edge.

Mike Freedman

Acknowledgments

This book would not have been possible without the help of many friends, colleagues, and, most of all, the senior executives with whom I have worked. They are too numerous to mention but they know who they are. Extra special thanks are due to Mary Frintner, whose editing was invaluable, to literary agent Peter Tobia of Market Access, who challenged my thinking, and to Bruce Keener for moral and financial support. Above all, my thanks to Ben Tregoe and John Zimmerman whose initial thinking on strategic leadership inspired me to join Kepner-Tregoe. Other Kepner-Tregoe colleagues who have given valuable advice and input include Alan Brache, Roger Miller, and Bill Shine (North America); David Choo (Southeast Asia); Philip Curra (Francophone Europe); Jim Edson (Australia); Sam Bodley-Scott and Andrew Graham (United Kingdom); and Hajime Nakajima (Japan).

It has been both a privilege and a sometimes scary responsibility to be involved in helping to shape the future of so many fine organizations, their employees, customers, suppliers, and other constituencies. Many thanks to those at the coalface who have let me share their experiences in the awesome and often daunting task of thinking strategically.

Last but not least I am indebted to my family for the faith, support, and encouragement they have given me during this project. It would not have been completed without their understanding.

Introduction

The need for honest strategic leadership has never been more important. The twenty-first century demands, as has no other, that corporate leaders create both strategic literacy and a robust process to ensure strategic constancy. In this critical work of setting, implementing, reviewing, and updating strategy, both art and discipline must be applied with passion, skill, and commitment. These strengths ensure at least a fighting chance of survival and make possible the levels of success demanded by all the stakeholders in an organization.

Every corporate leader faces new challenges. CEOs and their top teams must quickly develop the ability to fend off traditional competitors who are becoming fiercer, resist unrecognizable and unanticipated forms of new competition, reinvent their organizations in the face of new technologies, and meet shifts in their value chains and new industry paradigms. And they must do so at a tempo that matches the breakneck speed of the many changes to the environment in which every organization operates.

This book presents a thought-provoking, integrated, and proven approach to strategy that meets these imperatives head on and challenges chief executives, their top teams, and future leaders to benchmark their strategic effectiveness. The book also provides breakthrough concepts and processes to help improve strategic performance, arguably the most important aspect of a top team's work.

The foundation of this book is the unique five-phase model for strategy formulation and implementation developed by Kepner-Tregoe.

Based in Princeton, New Jersey, Kepner-Tregoe, Inc., is a management consulting firm specializing in strategic and operational decision making. The efficacy of the Kepner-Tregoe model has been demonstrated in a wide variety of public, private, and not-for-profit organizations from around the globe.

Too many books on strategy are built on theory alone, and many are illustrated with only fictional examples, if at all. This book provides real examples of how the integrated approach advocated here has been deployed in some of the world's leading organizations. The book includes stories from the Bank of Ireland, British Airways, Corning, Crown Greetings, Hallmark International, the Hong Kong and China Gas Company Limited ("Towngas"), Kennametal, Lockheed Martin, the Royal Mail, the Savoy Group of Hotels, and the Labour Party.

Chapter 1 describes the need for strategic thinking and the art and discipline required to set, implement, and update strategy. Chapter 2 provides a holistic understanding of an organization as the backdrop for strategy, and it discusses the selection of the strategic leadership team members.

Chapters 3 through 12 describe and illustrate the five phases of strategy formulation and implementation. Chapter 3 examines the gathering and analysis of strategic intelligence for use as the basis of future decision making. It also discusses the need to avoid the "data overload" trap faced by twenty-first-century organizations.

Basic beliefs and values are an essential part of any organization's domain and an important foundation for guiding strategic choices. They are addressed in Chapter 4.

Chapters 5 and 6 outline a powerful process for creating alternative future visions, selecting the optimum one, refining it into a comprehensive strategy profile, and then deriving from that profile a matrix of products and markets that is the organization's roadmap throughout its strategic time frame.

Chapter 7 describes the key bridges between the strategic profile and its implementation. Chapter 8 is a discussion of the purpose, nature, and construct of a Strategic Master Project Plan, without which successful implementation is never a foregone conclusion.

Chapters 9 through 11 highlight the implementation cornerstones that are common to every enterprise. Organization structure, information, the product/market mix and its complexity, corporate culture, and people management must be aligned with the strategic intent. Communicating with all internal and external stakeholders is the basis for acceptance of the change inherent in strategy implementation.

Without continuous monitoring, reviewing, and updating, a strategy may quickly become outdated and potentially damaging. Chapter 12 looks at how strategy can remain "evergreen."

Chapter 13 explores the contingent world in which we live and conduct business and the emerging twenty-first-century trends that every strategic leader will have to address. The lessons gleaned from our work with strategic leaders over the past 20 years conclude the book in Chapter 14. From these deductions, chief executives and their colleagues will gain fresh insight into their own strategic performance on the stage of this already remarkable century.

On the Text

Wherever possible, clients whose strategic work is cited have been referred to by name. In some instances, however, to protect confidential information and respect a privileged relationship, clients are not identified. However, all such examples are factual accounts.

The words *organization, firm, company, enterprise,* and *business* are used interchangeably for the sake of literary variety.

Beyond Vision

In 1999 the future of mobile telephony in Europe seemed crystal clear. Telecommunications firms such as British Telecom, Vodaphone, and KPN and their suppliers Nokia, Motorola, Ericsson, and others bet much of their strategic future on 3G technology. By all accounts, a common commitment to 3G development would move cell phones into advanced mobile telephony, streaming video, and instant Internet access within a year or two. Between them, telecom firms committed over $100 billion to buy licenses for the game of technological leapfrog they anticipated.

In what appeared to be a case of strategic thinking at its best, the reality now is tough to swallow. As of this writing, 3G technology still lingers on a distant horizon. Vodaphone announced a loss of $20.9 billion for the financial year ending April 2002. Hamstrung by their own assumptions, companies have appealed to their governments to refund at least a portion of the hefty upfront fees collected—to no avail.

* * *

The top team of a global heavy-equipment manufacturer did its homework throughout the process of formulating a strategy. The result was mutual commitment to a clear vision, and implementation was a go.

In this firm, the president, a North American, was a powerful presence. His plan for communicating the strategy was simple; he would create a videotape to be sent simultaneously to every worldwide operation to educate employees and ensure their buy-in. But the video fell on (mostly) unreceptive eyes and ears. Small wonder, since few overseas employees spoke English, and even fewer found the president's American expressions and gestures familiar. The strategic message, critical for every player in the organization, was lost in an ineffective package.

Are the companies in these examples especially careless or even inept when it comes to strategy? No, not really. Most management teams are loyal and hardworking, and they have the best of strategic intentions. But their shortcomings are typical. Each failed in at least one critical aspect of the strategy process:

- In formulating a strategic vision based on facts, informed assumptions, and the best-possible what-if thinking
- In implementing and communicating the vision throughout the organization to clarify and align the role of every strategically critical player and process
- In monitoring and updating the vision to ensure its continued strength, agility, and relevance

Strategy is one of the most used and abused words in the corporate lexicon. Rarely will you find any two executives, consultants, or academics who agree on its definition. For us, strategy is the *framework of choices that determine the nature and direction of an organization.* The choices in the framework relate to what products and services will be offered and not offered, what markets will be served and not served, and what capabilities are needed to take products to markets.

What passes for strategic thinking in today's global economy is often dominated by the perceived potential—and recent disappointments—of dot.com frenzies, e-commerce, and mergers and acquisitions. Every industry segment has been overwhelmed by the merger mania of the past decade. Too often, strategic thought has been reduced to reactive decision making, gut feel, "me-too" policies, and short-termism aimed at pacifying shareholders and analysts. Although the longest boom in 100 years in North American and European stock markets helped to cushion the effects of ill-conceived strategies over the last decade, that boom and its decade are over.

In the time since the September 11 attacks, political and economic concerns have thrown a spotlight on strategic vulnerability. A climate of deep uncertainty and rapid change is the norm of the new century. Yet, unlike the pessimists who tout this uncertainty as a reason for abandoning strategic thought altogether, we believe strategy has never been more important.

Those who have announced the demise of strategy blame both external events and the nature of strategy itself. In such a climate, they argue that the very exercise of formulating a corporate strategy is outmoded, even irrelevant.

This book turns that thinking around. Now more than ever, the company that lacks a coherent strategy is vulnerable. But the company that has a clear direction and then squanders it through shoddy implementation is equally at risk.

STRATEGIC THINKING: ART AND DISCIPLINE

A crucial lesson we have learned over many years of strategy engagements is that strategic leadership requires a combination of art and discipline. By art, we mean thinking that is creative, out of the box, and blue sky. Examples include the creation of alternative strategic visions for top team assessment, new product development, the crafting of what-if scenarios, the identification of decision-making criteria, and the design of a new culture that is strategically aligned. Creativity is also required in other activities such as communicating the strategy and supporting ownership of and commitment to it.

The most dramatic and creative example of this kind of thinking we have ever seen came in our work with Hallmark International, the half-billion-dollar global subsidiary of Kansas City-based Hallmark Cards, Inc. During our discussion of potential new markets and products, a team member conceived of the cell phone greeting category—a quantum leap in its concept of format, delivery, content, and every other attribute of a greeting product. This breakthrough effort has already been launched in its first two markets under the newly formed subsidiary Crown Greetings Ltd.

Despite our focus on creativity, we do not preclude the requirement for other types of thinking such as those that are more rational and analytical. These have their equal place in the strategy process, as we will explore later.

Discipline is essential, both in the thought processes involved in strategy and in its execution. For example, it is not easy to craft and implement a plan that may include hundreds of projects and thousands of subprojects as the prerequisites to strategy implementation. Difficult too are the needs to ensure consistency of decision making throughout the organization; keep focused when so many options are available for consideration; and regularly to monitor, review, and update strategy when operational or financial imperatives are knocking at the door.

Nevertheless, leaders in a number of organizations have reaped rich rewards from the passionate belief in a disciplined approach to setting and implementing strategy.

LABOUR: STRATEGY FOR SURVIVAL

It's not often that an organization's failure to implement a powerful strategic vision could lead to its extinction in a single day. But in 1994, that's exactly what the Labour Party in the United Kingdom was up against if it failed to win the next general election.

Labour had not governed Britain for 15 years, and it had been defeated in four successive general elections. With the next election 3 years away, another defeat might have spelled the party's end. Such a result—the demise of not only a major political party but also the core of the nation's Labour movement—was unthinkable.

Tony Blair, the newly elected party leader, inherited a long-buried landmine. As a whole, the party machine was poorly staffed, badly managed, out of money, low in morale, and lacking respect in its 650 parliamentary districts around the country. Under Blair's three predecessors, it had achieved only marginal, reluctant change. Above all, the machine lacked a coherent vision of its role in both the Labour Party and the Labour movement as a whole.

Quite rightly, Blair was convinced that Labour would remain unelectable without a radical, strategic transformation he dubbed "modernization." The word meant much more to him than it implies. To support his political vision, nothing less was required than the most efficient, modern, motivated, disciplined, responsive, and proactive electoral organization in the world.

Within days, Blair invited Tom Sawyer to become the party's general secretary, a chief-executive equivalent. With a background in trade unions and a close familiarity with Labour, Sawyer had links to both direct stakeholders (party members, members of Parliament, and the structure nationwide) as well as to unions, cooperative societies, and socialist and social democratic parties in other nations.

Sawyer had mused with the author that "some of that strategy stuff" might make an excellent launching pad for his leadership. As far as possible, he and his top team used the five-phase model for strategy formulation and implementation described throughout this book. Their task—crafting and implementing a strategic vision within a political party machine—was no less difficult than it would be in a multi-billion-dollar global enterprise.

At Labour headquarters, Sawyer was forced to think carefully about getting the right team in place. Before formulating strategy, many of those in senior positions, especially with long years of service, had found it tough to think strategically, and even tougher to do so in a team environment. Few had experience in what Sawyer called "modern management tools and techniques," not even in the basics of project management or process improvement. They were in alien territory; some did not survive, while others rose to the occasion. Similarly, newcomers were not easily integrated into an organization with such an inbred culture and style; some rejected the machine, while others were rejected by it.

Over time, the survivors learned to think the unthinkable, dump a lot of baggage, improve their strategic judgment, and accept radical change in the form of a clear strategic vision. They became convinced that they could create the ultimate election machine.

At the core of the vision was the clarification of who the customers of the party machine were. Top management knew the answer to this instinctively, but it had never codified its understanding, nor had it clarified the relative importance of customer groups. The party machine had to understand the needs and expectations of each discrete customer group and then direct its priorities and focus toward developing the services to meet those needs, and the capabilities to deliver those services. The range of customers was diverse. It included party members, elected representatives (including members of Parliament, local councillors, members of the European Parliament), candidates for parliamentary seats held by the opposition, the National Executive Committee, the shadow cabinet, affiliated organizations (trade unions, cooperative societies, and pressure groups), local political agents and voluntary officials, and the media. Most importantly, the electorate was to be treated as a customer in its own right.

The range of services to be offered to these customers was equally large and diverse. It included information, policy research and advice, political education, training for party workers, public and press relations, legal and constitutional services, conference organization, and the production and printing of election materials.

Eventually, top management in the party machine crafted its vision to address these requirements, and it framed the vision within a set of basic beliefs that was used to guide the behavior of the party's employees.

It was not easy. Staff members throughout the party frequently worked as a "labour of love," often at considerable personal cost, and they were set in their ways. Accustomed to a cagey culture of internal politicking, they weren't natural team players, preferring the comfort of their own territory. Even the water-cooler talk centered on past failures; a vision of success was fundamentally foreign. But the top team persisted in modeling a clear strategic mindset, in communicating the strategic importance—or irrelevance—of certain activities, and in operating with common purpose across the whole organization.

Communicating the vision and gaining ownership and commitment to it—from Tony Blair to every party employee—was vital. As a start, the first meeting in living memory was held at which all regional directors in the field met with all the headquarters staff.

The party's strategic focus and its implementation were made visible, for example, in the establishment of its Key Seats department, targeting 100 marginal parliamentary constituencies and forcing attention away from internal staff matters to party members and voters. Candidates in these constituencies became the highest-priority customer category. If the party were to win each of these seats and retain current ones, Labour would govern again.

Recognizing the strategic importance of communicating Labour's position to the electorate, the party machine created a powerful communication vehicle called the Rebuttal Unit. This unit developed an Internet-based library of information with which to take the initiative in responding swiftly to political events and gaining coverage for the non-ruling party on the day's political news. The party also undertook a massive effort to improve the skills of its employees through the government-sponsored Investors in People program, focusing, for example, on project management and related processes to secure the strategy's successful implementation.

In short, the machine was transformed; the landslide results of the 1997 general election testified to that. This creation of "New Labour" by Blair has been well documented. It succeeded in no small measure because Sawyer and his team formulated a clear vision and met the implementation barriers head on.

STRATEGIC LEADERS: GOING THE DISTANCE

In this book are stories of others who, like Tom (now Lord) Sawyer, set out on the journey with great personal strengths in strategic thinking. It is the chief executive's role to model this commitment to strategic thinking in order to motivate others. A leader's discipline in profound, rational, and creative thinking is what encourages teams to embrace radical change.

Discipline keeps strategic vision from becoming an unmet aspiration; it is key to ensuring implementation so that vision becomes reality.

Over the last several years, the top team at Hallmark International, led by Keith Alm, CEO of this worldwide subsidiary of Hallmark Cards Inc., formulated and implemented strategy. Alm was an experienced strategist and unrelenting in his insistence on a strategy process that would lead to the continuous development of his leadership team. When Alm was asked to join Hallmark to address the slump in international business, he already knew the process should be one of ongoing education.

Alm assembled his top team by weeding through those who had been promoted on the basis of operational excellence to find natural—or educable—strategic thinkers. He made a strong commitment to a disciplined framework for strategy, ensuring its results by avoiding shortcuts to the overall process. And implementation began with extensive training in planning, decision making, project management, and other strategy-related skills for hundreds of employees around the world.

When Alfred Chan was appointed managing director of the Hong Kong and China Gas Company Limited ("Towngas") in 1997, he too faced an uphill battle. Given Hong Kong's reintegration into China, a swiftly changing customer base, and a tired, nonentrepreneurial group of employees, Chan didn't leap to short-term solutions. Instead, he committed to a holistic, iterative strategic process.

First, he led the way in gathering information about Towngas customers and markets by observing and participating in the day-to-day business—even cooking in customers' kitchens. Having educated himself and his top team, he then led the reframing of the company's strategic vision. And finally, he set out to transform the underlying culture of the entire change-averse organization. Only after these three goals were accomplished did Chan and his team turn to improving the company's organization structure and business processes. A-to-Z commitment to strategy helped Chan engineer the Towngas turnaround by 1999.

AVOIDING STRATEGY BY DEFAULT

The brave efforts required of these successful leaders—Tom Sawyer, Keith Alm, Alfred Chan, and many others we have worked with—are proof that this work is not for the fainthearted. All too often, a senior team shirks its commitment to the time and resources needed to do it right. But without such commitment, the organization will be overwhelmed with a strategy by default.

Whether you know it or not, your organization already has some semblance of direction—just as it already has products, markets, business processes, a corporate culture, an organization structure, and a reward system. The origins of a corporate strategy may be like those of a company's products or markets; it may be inherited, stumbled into, borrowed from a competitor or holding company, or even nearly invisible. In every organization, there are "bottom-up" assumptions about strategy that ultimately guide critical choices in all areas. An ad hoc strategy can expose your company to the following threats:

Your competitors: In today's accelerated time frames, they'll be ahead before you know it. Even in comparatively stable markets, your competitive strengths are a moving target. No competitor will wait patiently until you've reestablished your strategic priorities; they're too busy getting on with their own.

The chances that your competitive advantage will be sustainable for long periods are diminishing rapidly; its shelf life is more dependent than ever on factors beyond your control.

We worked with an electronics company that had developed the first radio pager in the 1960s, then a technological coup. Yet the company eventually became stalled on strategic intent, unable to define where its invention of the radio pager might lead. It didn't take long for companies like Motorola and Sony to grab the technology leadership from this smaller firm and exploit it to their own advantage. The well-documented strategic scramblings of Xerox and IBM in the 1970s and 1980s are other examples of companies that have fallen into this trap.

Your shareholders: Short-termism is seductive, yet potentially fatal. It is no secret that some top executives in recent years have either pandered to or been overwhelmed by the perceived need for short-term earnings growth, often pursuing such gains in ways that precluded a well-conceived strategy. In addition, the stock option incentives awarded to many executives actually compromised their strategic leadership. Gordon Gekko's famous words in the movie *Wall Street* have been disproved: Greed is *not* good for you. The recent scandals involving previous stock market stars like Enron, Tyco, WorldCom, and Xerox come to mind as examples of poor and dishonest leadership. In another type of short-termism, mergers and acquisitions have often proved to be disastrous substitutes for strategic thinking in the quest for growth and short-term profits. Examples include Xerox's acquisition of an insurance company, divested some years later, and the multi-billion-dollar purchase of Fortis by U.K. giant Marconi, which only months later was forced to write off Fortis's assets to zero.

The real issue? No chief executive is able to take command of the organization without a clear and shared vision of the future.

It is not the purpose of this book to argue against the need for profits, even in the short term. However, most organizations find that short-term gains are no guarantee of future success. The world is not a static place, and today's star products or markets may well be tomorrow's busts. But when assumptions about that world are understood and leveraged strategically, the odds of success are clearly better.

Your own employees: Driven to "do something," their operational focus may force their hand on answering the "how" without having defined the "what." An operational bias may pervade the organization with quick fixes, compromises, and a lack of cohesion. Or, as a member of the top strategic team of the Savoy Group of Hotels snapped at its first strategy meeting, "Never mind this strategic thinking business. Let's get rid of the f---ing cockroaches!"

This knee-jerk focus is tempting because it addresses how to get things done—seductive in the short term. But, as at the Savoy, executives are often tempted to escalate the cockroach wars without remembering the "what" that forms the very reason for the organization's being. In the Savoy's case, this was the vision of an outstanding hotel and restaurant service for its guests—or more broadly, of a strong market position among senior business travelers and high-net-worth individuals.

Just as treacherous is the vacuum that evolves when strategic vision is weak or missing in action. We worked once with a small manufacturer, 40 percent of whose sales were to the behemoth retailer Home Depot. As a company, the manufacturer was unclear about the strategic implications of its supplier role. Consequently, most of its decisions were dictated by Home Depot's needs, even when those decisions were not a good fit for the company's other customers or its future direction.

The strategic vulnerability of such a vacuum is clear. It breeds inaction, indecision, and a state of animated suspension. No central purpose brings employees, functions, or business units together. Resources are spread thin and allocated to squeaky wheels. Initiative fatigue sets in, as operational measures fall flat. In such a vacuum the organization's future will eventually be held in hostile hands.

MAKING THE COMMITMENT

Top management's task is to choose, implement, and then continuously monitor the correct strategy. Without active engagement in this process, an organization will founder in the wake of external forces that shape its progress. The chief executive and team who refuse to make this ongoing commitment will find themselves at the mercy of the prevailing economic, political, and competitive winds.

A word of caution: Strategy takes time. It takes courage. It would be much easier to delegate the task and have answers delivered on a silver platter. But ask yourself: Is strategic thinking a function I can afford to outsource or delegate? We hope that, in this book, we can convince you that commitment from the top is the vital link to a robust, workable, and successful strategy.

2

Strategic Leadership: What It Really Takes

Perhaps against our better judgment, we once worked with a company that seemed highly motivated by the strategy process. The team was well meaning, the need for strategy more than obvious. There was just one catch: The CEO refused to be involved. His instruction was to have the top team meet, work through the formulation process, craft a strategic vision—and then bring the result to him for his approval or rejection. He alone, as he informed us, would let us know whether the team had "got it right."

Needless to say, the team's efforts and subsequent implementation were in jeopardy before they began.

When an organization is about to take on the work of strategy, the chief executive must be out in front. This chapter will look at the key questions chief executives should be asking themselves—and answering—before strategy formulation can begin:

- Where in the organization does strategy unfold? What is the playing field?
- How do I define what strategy is and clarify the process for getting there?
- How will I lead my team? Who will be my key players—and who will serve us better from the sideline?

KNOWING YOUR PLAYING FIELD:
THE ENTERPRISE MODEL

Leaders know intuitively that strategy impacts every critical area of an organization. Let's define more closely the playing field upon which strategy unfolds.

The Enterprise Model shown in Figure 2-1 appears in the recently published book *How Organizations Work: Taking a Holistic Approach to Enterprise Health*, written by our colleague Alan Brache.[1] This 360-degree view portrays the critical areas for change and performance improvement in an organization; they are as interdependent as the various organs and systems of a living organism. It also shows the broad-ranging impact of the decisions made and actions taken throughout strategy formulation and implementation.

The work of an organization, the "business of the business," lies expressly in the position it occupies in a given value chain between its suppliers and other resources (*upstream*) and its customers and other constituencies (*downstream*). Formulating a strategy is the platform from which a company defines its current place in the value chain and carves out the portion of the value chain in which it will participate in the future. This definition ideally distinguishes the organization from its competitors' role in a similar value chain. In some radical instances, the formulation of strategy may dramatically redefine the value chain itself (for example, the Internet's impact on delivery of goods and services in the business-to-consumer arena, which may eliminate an intermediary distributor altogether).

In the first phase of strategy formulation, external variables and influences are assessed, as described in Chapter 3. They include the following:

- *Environmental variables*: The expectations of governmental and regulatory bodies, the local and global communities where the organization operates, economic and technological trends, threats and opportunities, and trends in society at large.
- *Shareholders and the parent company*: The mutual relationship between the company and those who contribute to its financial strength and profit from its financial gains.
- *Customers and markets*: The mutual relationship between those who have needs that are potentially fulfilled by the organization and the products and services that might meet those needs.

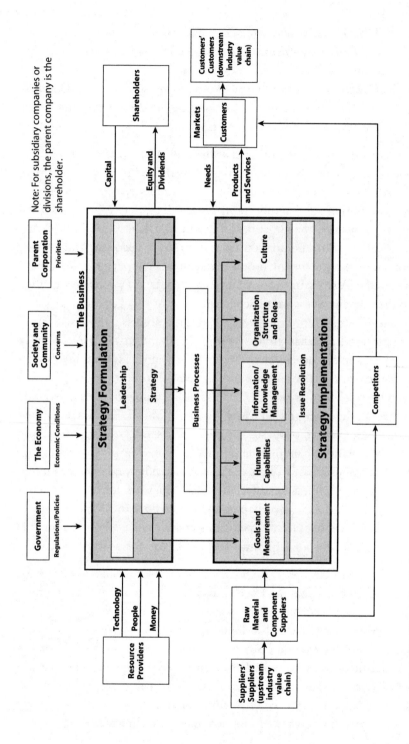

Note: For subsidiary companies or divisions, the parent company is the shareholder.

Figure 2-1 The Enterprise Model

- *Suppliers and resource providers*: The external sources of raw materials and components, as well as technology, people, capital, and even wholly outsourced capabilities.
- *Competitors*: Others engaged in creating similar value. Competition occurs both upstream (for suppliers/resources) and downstream (for customers/markets).

The internal variables shown in the Enterprise Model constitute the components of the organization as it creates value. Foremost among these is strategy formulation. Any sound strategic vision will be based on assumptions and implications about the external variables listed above; however, the organization's strategic legacy also has certain implications. An examination of past strategic successes and failures, including the pursuit of product and market opportunities, complements the close examination of existing beliefs and values to contribute to the framework for strategic vision.

As an organization prepares for future success, no internal factors are more critical than strategy formulation and its *leadership*. Leadership—visioning, developing, motivating, communicating, involving—is the real horsepower of successful strategy formulation.

Once strategy is set, the success of its implementation is at the mercy of the organization's *issue resolution systems*. The quality, effectiveness, and speed of these shared processes and structures for applying information, gaining commitment, exploiting opportunities, and turning away threats will move the organization from vision to implementation. The elements of a common framework for issue resolution are discussed later in this chapter and throughout the book.

The remaining internal factors, listed here and addressed more fully in Chapters 6 through 10, must also be aligned for strategic success:

- *Business processes:* The processes that describe how work is done, both those that interface with customers and suppliers and those that are more internally focused.
- *Goals*: The financial and nonfinancial measures of success derived from the strategy, both as overall business objectives and as specific measures cascaded down through the organization, that support the assessment of team and individual performance.
- *Human capabilities*: The skills and knowledge of the workforce, which may be of a process, content, or technical nature.

- *Organization structure*: The formal grouping of responsibilities and the reporting hierarchy, most often designed around function, geography, customers, products, SBUs, or processes.
- *Information/knowledge management*: The data that are collected and subsequently analyzed, disseminated, and applied in support of the organization's value creation.
- *Culture*: The combined effect of behaviors, values, heritage, thinking, and relationships and the way these are embedded in an organization and its performance.

Each of these variables impacts, and is impacted by, the choices made during strategy formulation. The tasks undertaken to address each area constitute the strategy's implementation. When an organization embarks on the path to strategic change, the alignment of these variables with its strategy is critical.

The next step for any chief executive setting out on this journey is to understand the strategic task more precisely.

UNDERSTANDING THE STRATEGIC FRAMEWORK

What Strategy Is

As noted in the previous chapter, strategy is the *framework of choices that determine the nature and direction of an organization.*

The *framework* as a whole establishes the boundaries or parameters that define the scope of business activity—in short, an organization's domain. The screens, or criteria, that determine what's "in" or "out" are derived from a variety of sources, such as the current domain, the organization's overriding beliefs and values, the competitive advantages identified, and shareholder and parent company interests.

For example, a privately owned Swiss trading firm, Gerad S.A., does not trade with terrorist regimes or their supporters; they also choose not to trade in weapons, tobacco, or alcohol. These activities would contradict the core beliefs of its devout Hindu owners.

Choices are made in three dimensions of the organization: the products and services that it will offer, the markets (customers, consumers, and geographies) that it will serve, and the key capabilities that it must deploy in order to take its products and services to its markets.

The criteria that guide these choices vary. We know of several global firms, for example, that have chosen to limit their entry into certain geographic markets based on the prevalence of an acceptable business climate characterized by a solid banking structure, minimal corruption, a minimum per capita gross domestic product (GDP), and an overall Western legal and business orientation.

The *nature* of an organization is what exemplifies it, describes its character, and makes its shape recognizable. For example, McDonald's is now the epitome of a "fast-food chain." Around the world, Intel means "chips," and Disney is synonymous with "family entertainment." The nature of an organization lends strategic coherence to its decision making and communication.

Of course, a strategy also has much to say about the future. *Direction* is our term for the organization's future course. It encompasses the choices that will be made about future products and services, future customers and markets. For example, McDonald's could once have been described as a "hamburger chain," but that no longer applies. Through ongoing strategic choices about its direction, its nature has been redefined. Ford and other automobile companies have metamorphosed to encompass both products (agricultural equipment, even airplanes) and services (insurance, financing, and rental/leasing) that redefine their nature. Is BMW now a "transport company"? Daimler-Chrysler a "conglomerate"?

Every organization has a direction; it is headed somewhere. Unfortunately, in many organizations, that direction is not the result of a conscious choice. The best organizations are led by chief executives who have the insight and the discipline to ensure that the use of an effective process leads the organization in a clearly defined direction.

In a sense, organizations continually reinvent themselves as they make strategic choices. New markets may be pursued as certain criteria are relaxed, tightened, or revised; older products may be abandoned as the overall framework shifts based on new technological assumptions. This constant evaluation of what is in and what is out is a reflection of a shift in a dynamic strategy. Whether these changes are transformational or incremental, they arise as a result of the organization's strategic framework.

What Strategy Is Not

Many senior executives hold the erroneous view that, if an issue is long term, it is strategic; if short term, it is tactical or operational. They confuse duration with strategic importance. Long-range planning, for example, is primarily a financially oriented exercise in most organizations; its focus reflects and anticipates the results to be achieved through strategic choices but does not constitute the strategy itself.

Similarly, if a decision is large, involving, for example, a multi-million-dollar expenditure, it may or may not be strategic. Even the acquisition of a rival to pursue additional products, markets, or capabilities may not be considered strategic if the essential framework remains unchanged.

This is not to say, of course, that planning and other operational issues are not closely linked to strategy or are unimportant. Indeed, their strategic alignment is crucial. But the questions they address are of a quite different nature. Strategy is concerned with what an organization aims to be, and why. Operations constitute the how of getting there.

Organizations that have a clearly defined strategy but are weak operationally will need to determine whether their strategy is indeed correct, or whether a quantum leap in operational effectiveness is required. Those that attain short-term operational excellence without a coherent strategic vision run the risk of arriving—at the wrong destination—more quickly than expected.[2]

A chief executive's understanding of the distinction between strategy and operations will bring into clear focus the difficult tasks of his or her formulation and implementation teams. Effective strategy setting does not lend itself to magic-bullet thinking. No single concept—not Hamel's core competencies approach or his current mantra of broad involvement, not Porter's now-ubiquitous competitive advantage, not the content knowledge, scenario-driven approaches of strategy boutiques like McKinsey or the Boston Consulting Group—will take the place of answering these nine central questions that form the core of a strategic vision.

Asking the Right Questions in Constructing the Strategic Framework

In their quest to create a clear strategy, the best strategic leaders will consciously seek answers to these nine questions:

1. What are the assumptions about various aspects of the external environment (demographic, economic, political, competitive) and internal environment that will guide our strategic decision making? What are the implications for our organization of each of these?

2. What are the fundamental beliefs and values that guide how we do business?
3. Which products and/or services will we offer, and not offer?
4. Which customer and/or end-user groups will we serve, and not serve?
5. Which geographic markets will we serve, and not serve?
6. Which products and markets represent the greatest potential for growth? Which require the most significant investment?
7. Which competitive advantage(s) will enable us to succeed?
8. Which key capabilities must we have to take our products to our markets and support our competitive advantage(s)?
9. What financial and nonfinancial results do we aim to achieve?

These questions are few in number but powerful in application. Their answers constitute the framework for developing the vision, implementing it, and guiding its ongoing renewal.

CHOOSING A PROCESS FOR STRATEGY ENGAGEMENT

Finally, a chief executive must choose the most effective strategy-setting process for his or her organization. In today's volatile world, having a robust process to guide strategy formulation and implementation is nearly as important as the content of the strategy itself.

Two criteria should influence the CEO in making this critical choice of strategic process: the fundamental nature of the process itself and the specific steps suggested for moving an organization through the process. Any sound strategy process should be based on a systematic questioning approach; it should also include, in some form, the five steps of analysis, formulation, planning, implementation, and review.

The Nature of the Process: The Power of Systematic Questioning

As described above, the task of strategy formulation is to seek answers to the nine key questions about the nature and direction of the business. Let's consider here what might best characterize that search.

First is this: Strategy is built around the answers to a vital few questions, rather than masses of data. Typically, consultants from a traditional strategy boutique might pose a hypothesis—for example, about growth or product leadership—and then undertake massive studies to prove its validity. There is an unfortunate assumption implicit in this approach—that the top executives of an organization know less than their consultants do. This just doesn't square with our experience. The vast majority of top teams we've encountered know their industry, their markets, and their value chain more intimately than outsiders ever could.

If there are significant gaps in the strategic intelligence and knowledge of an organization, and most specifically among the members of its top team, there may be a need to fill these, either internally under guided facilitation, or through the use of external sources to provide the information—but *not* to set the strategy.

Although factual research can be helpful in assessing external variables, there is plenty of room for common sense and judgment. If details about a particular market are required to make critical decisions, we promote the gathering of that data and the analysis needed to make good strategic judgments. Most often, however, members of the top team are perfectly well informed about the particular trends and quandaries of their businesses.

It may not even be the content experts who have the most to offer. In the early 1990s, Jim Breisinger was the financial controller for consumable industrial tooling giant Kennametal Inc.; he was called to Europe to bring operations there under a single umbrella. Clearly, it wasn't content expertise that defined his leadership. There, as he led his team through setting strategy, he quickly acknowledged that "the people who were in these European businesses obviously knew more about them than I did. At that point, it was process questioning that could bring people together very quickly and very efficiently in charting a future course and forming a cohesive business unit."

We believe it is more effective to set the top team to work on the vital few strategic questions than to have them mull over detailed data or the hypotheses of their consultants. Soon enough, this focus on a set of systematic questions will reveal any data gaps that must be filled in order for the team to reach sound conclusions. And when leaders insist that the team focus on these questions, they nurture the development of strategic thinking skills in the organization.

Second: Solid process questions will yield greater strategic dividends than narrowly focused, content-driven questions. We believe that exploring some types of questions yields far greater dividends than exploring others. Consider this example: A strategy team, contemplating expansion of its African markets, might pose these content questions:

- When should we enter the sub-Saharan marketplace?
- Which countries in that marketplace should we go into first?

Now consider these process questions about the same decision:

- Should we pursue growth through entering new geographic markets in Africa?
- What are the criteria we should use for selecting new markets?
- Which alternative markets should be considered?
- Does the sub-Saharan market meet our criteria better than other alternatives?
- Which factors have influenced the success of our previous market forays?
- What potential problems might we encounter?

These questions are much more powerful and useful than those that are content oriented. A process approach to identifying and resolving issues involves a logical sequence of steps to gather, organize, and analyze information. We call this *rational process*. It has the advantage of being universal since it is independent of the context in which it is applied. It allows for analytical and creative thinking. Properly applied, the questions that stem from it leave no place for executives to hide. Adopting such a common approach throughout the strategy process enhances the probability of success not least because there is a shared understanding of the logic behind the strategic thought process and the resulting conclusions. As Keith Alm says, "It is the mix of rational analysis and creative juices that makes the process so powerful. Our facilitators asked tough questions and stimulated out-of-the-box thinking."

Strategy implementation, as well as formulation, will be enhanced by the use of rational processes for making decisions, solving problems, and analyzing potential problems and opportunities. These processes also form the cornerstone of the issue resolution component of the Enterprise Model.[3]

Third: The success of strategy formulation and implementation depends on the skill and commitment of the top team. We do not arrive with a predetermined preference for a strategic alternative. Our role is to assist clients in crafting their strategy in response to the key questions. In that very difficult task, top teams find that a systematic, rational process not only improves the quality of their strategic vision but helps to cement the commitment needed to carry it through.

Rational process provides the team with a common vocabulary to cut through the semantics of words—and politics—that may drive them apart. Within the framework of a common language, participants can make their best personal contributions. With a sequence of powerful questions, participants are able to disengage from the hidden agendas and power plays that plague many senior teams.

Most importantly, this level of participation in frank, focused debate on the toughest questions brings a team tremendous pride and ownership in the common vision they forge. And that ownership is the foundation for the unwavering commitment that will be required of them to succeed in implementation.

The importance of this strategic cohesion cannot be underestimated. In 1996, when the Bank of Ireland acquired Bristol and West Bank, it was in large part the strength of the Bristol and West's top-to-bottom commitment to their recently crafted strategy that distinguished them from other candidates, impressed their buyers, and sealed the deal.

The Roadmap: The Five Phases of Strategy Formulation and Implementation

At this point, the challenge becomes: What are the critical steps for setting and implementing strategy? How will we get from where we are today to where we'd like to be in the future? Figure 2-2 outlines the five phases of work for addressing the strategic dimension of an enterprise. We discuss briefly the activities of each phase below; Chapters 3 to 12 are devoted to examining each in greater detail.

Phase 1. Strategic Intelligence Gathering and Analysis

In Phase 1 an organization's executives assess the present and likely future trends in markets, competition, technology, regulations, and economic conditions. They also examine certain internal variables: the

Figure 2-2   The Five Phases of Formulating and Implementing Strategy

organization's values, capabilities, product and market results, and past strategic endeavors. The strength of the assessment depends on the depth and breadth of the information examined, as well as the ability of the top team to draw valid conclusions. The team develops a set of assumptions about the future, the resulting implications for the organization, and a profile of the environment in which strategic decisions will be made.

Phase 2. Strategy Formulation
Based on the Phase 1 outputs, the top team examines alternative futures and then selects and creates the strategic profile or vision, addressing the nine key questions of strategy formulation mentioned earlier. The quality of the formulation depends on the strength of the process through which the team makes these decisions, as well as the strategic capabilities of the team's members.

Phase 3. Strategic Master Project Planning
Based on the strategic vision, a significant number of projects emerge, often several hundred; these are the tasks that must be completed to

ensure successful strategy implementation. Using sophisticated project management methods, a plan for how these projects will be clarified, prioritized, sequenced, scheduled, resourced, executed, and monitored is created. Projects that will have the most significant impact may be identified in an optimal project portfolio. Overall, the strength of implementation planning depends on the relevance of the actions chosen to convert strategic decisions to operational reality and on the quality of the project management process.

Such projects will span diverse activities. A new product launch may require, for example, information technology support, amended performance expectations for product developers, even a shift in the organization's structure to foster collaboration. To fill a capability gap, a project to identify an outsourcing solution or an acquisition may be needed.

Phase 4. Strategy Implementation

With a well-crafted plan in hand, implementation begins. Several elements affect its success. Foremost, of course, is the quality of project execution. Every plan also requires a major communications effort and broad employee involvement; many will include significant training in issue resolution skills. Throughout, the progress of each project is systematically reviewed, and modifications are made as necessary.

Phase 5. Strategy Monitoring, Reviewing, and Updating

To ensure its continuing efficacy, the strategy must be monitored regularly. Phase 5 (not really a phase at all, but an ongoing way of doing business) includes the review of both internal indicators—progress against strategic goals and measures, and progress on implementation projects—as well as of external indicators, that is, the continuing validity of basic assumptions upon which the vision was created.

Feedback comes from many sources: long-range planning and budgeting activities; ongoing operational projects that compete for key resources; communication with employees, customers, and suppliers; and the progress made on implementation projects.

At Hallmark International, the top team understands the importance of securing strategic continuity. "Very few people understand," says Alm, "the commitment made by our senior leadership to ensure that the strategic process doesn't have a start or finish. We do a complete review once or twice a year, but it's not a one-time activity."

The Iterative Construct

Strategy is never a linear, one-time effort. At any point in the five phases, new information will enable the team to ensure the strategy's continuous renewal. Key decision points are revisited. A strategy must never be isolated from the outside world or from internal activities vital to an organization's success.

From the description of these phases, it is clear how much time and attention must be devoted to strategic activities—and not just by the top team. As an iterative process, it broadens the strategic dimension of the jobs of most management and executive employees—something we find is needed in most companies.

PUTTING THE TEAM IN PLACE

Finally, the chief executive must assemble his or her team, optimally made up of 8 to 12 members. Though many criteria play a role in the choice of team members, the following are some of the most important:

> *The appropriate people:* Are your prospective members working at the highest levels, with significant responsibility? Will their leadership inspire a large segment of the organization? Do they have the right distribution of expertise? Have you included those who "should" be involved, while making room for the unexpected but creative contributor?
>
> *Good judgment:* Have you identified team members who are able to move beyond systematic, fact-based analysis to act on their best instincts and judgment? As the chief executive, do you trust their judgment? Doug Todd, managing director of Crown Greetings (a Hallmark subsidiary), admits that he requires detailed analyses from managers whose judgment he finds shaky or knows too little about. Yet, if he knows that an individual has subjected information to rational thinking processes, Todd may be willing to act without knowing all of the details. Strategy formulation puts a premium on visionaries who also have a firm grip on reality.
>
> *Passion and courage:* These qualities distinguish those who lead from those who manage. Later in the process, financial planners and operational managers will have their day. But in formulating

strategy, team members must accept assumptions that are rapidly shifting, overcome time frames that are impossibly brief, and prepare for the worst. You want team members who thrive on these challenges.

Collaboration: Team members will need to balance their passion to persuade with the grace to compromise. At the end of the day, they must be willing to accept the outcome of a rational process and their collective wisdom, put politics aside, and commit to the solidarity of the team.

And above all, strategic thinking ability: Along with most senior leaders, we believe there are mental attributes that predispose individuals toward this intellectual work. Those best suited to the task have the following:

- *Conceptual strength:* The ability to think incisively and systematically about abstract matters.
- *A holistic perspective:* The ability to see the whole picture without being constrained or misled by its various parts.
- *Creativity:* The ability to think out of the box, to come up with radically new ideas, and to move beyond existing constructs.
- *Expressiveness:* The ability to translate abstract thinking about the organization into clear words and pictures that are understood by others.
- *Tolerance for ambiguity:* The ability to analyze effectively even when the information available is incomplete or conflicting, or when there is great pressure to adopt a particular solution.
- *A sense of stewardship for the future:* The willingness to consider options that may sacrifice short-term gain to protect the organization's resources over time.

The alternative, of course, is to hire a strategy consultant to do the team's thinking for it. That was an option Keith Alm of Hallmark International never considered.

Says Alm, "I had no desire for a band of consultants from New York, New Jersey, and the United Kingdom to come in and solve my problems for me. I wanted my managing directors to find the solutions 'within,' so that they really owned them. And to do that, they had to start thinking strategically."

Putting together the strategy team was no easy task for Alm. Hired from outside Hallmark, he took on responsibility for every non–U.S. Hallmark operation. Alm himself was an experienced strategist, but the potential team was a different story.

Alm reviewed his existing leadership constituency; most were the managing directors of their operations. Several new people who came on board through recent acquisitions had to be included as well. Over the next 3 months, he met with this "first-cut" team to begin walking through the strategy process.

Alm says:

> **The process gave me a chance to observe who was embracing [strategic thinking], who wanted to take it forward, who was rejecting it, and who was getting lost in it. We were able to determine who could be brought up to speed, whose participation was not productive, and whose role would be deferred until the long-range planning process. We turned over roughly a third of those we started with, and we brought new members in. Our single point of focus was that everyone at the table had to be a leader. The only other criterion was that they not be engaged in managing a crisis or critical project whose failure would really damage us.**

Among the qualities Alm found lacking in those who couldn't think strategically were these: no generation of new ideas, no forethought regarding dynamics in their own markets, no relationship to the consumer, and a penchant for adapting North American practices to the local marketplace through intuition alone.

The chief executive is instrumental in the team's success. Often, he or she is the one who can suggest which individuals might work well together or how a newcomer's observations or skills can inform the process. Most importantly, he or she role-models the art and discipline required by demonstrating tolerance for creativity and insisting on a disciplined approach to inform the team's collective judgment.

STRATEGIC LEADERSHIP IN ACTION

Keith Alm's will for strategic action fits the profile of other successful chief executives with whom we have worked. He was relatively new to his job at Hallmark International, took the helm when the international business had been eroding for a number of years, and had an urgent need to "understand what my resource structure was like and the capabilities of my people."

Like other smart chief executives, Alm understood that embarking on strategy formulation would give his team a chance to reflect on their overall nature and direction, to assess their potential for strategic leadership, and to unite behind a clear process and a coherent vision. It's no surprise that nearly half our engagements are done with top executives who have been in their positions for less than a year.

Alm also moved quickly from stemming the operational hemorrhage to the strategic reinvention of his business. Victor Rice, who served as CEO of the agricultural equipment giant Massey-Ferguson (and its successor companies, Varity and Lucas Varity) in the 1980s and 1990s, faced a similar challenge. There, in a situation that could have resulted in Canada's largest-ever bankruptcy, top management gave their absolute commitment to the time and resources required for strategic renewal. At times when the payroll was barely met, the senior team worked tirelessly to balance their day-to-day operational imperatives with the work of strategy formulation.

That team embodied the leadership required. So can yours. But first, it will need your commitment to these critical tasks: clearly understanding the organization's internal and external drivers; agreeing to a common definition of strategy and the key questions it will answer; selecting a comprehensive process that ensures the strategic vision will not gather dust in a drawer; and assembling a team that will be diligent in pursuing excellence in strategic thinking.

3

From Data to Wisdom

More than once, at our first meeting, a chief executive has proudly pulled a 151-page, 4-inch-thick binder from his drawer, filled with data from public sources on demographic trends and the latest technological developments, or even the company's own return rates on its most recent marketing campaign. "We don't need to do any additional intelligence gathering or analysis before we set strategy," he may say. "It's all right here."

Contrast that with the firm hands-on approach Alfred Chan adopted when he took the reins at Towngas in 1997. Chan eschewed the hefty trend reports and donned coveralls to accompany technicians on customer calls. He challenged his top team to a competition on unfamiliar turf—literally cooking with gas to produce tasty dishes on a limited budget. He put senior executives out on the front line selling Towngas appliances in shopping mall showrooms. Only when Chan was satisfied that he and his team understood Towngas's customer relationships did he deem them ready to *address the future of the organization. "You have to go to the front line and observe what is happening," he explains. No 4-inch-thick binder for him!*

The data that top executives so readily present as their ticket out of this phase of the strategy process is simply that—data. It's typically in-digestible, historical, overwhelmingly detailed, focused on the financials—

and almost never a reflection of the thinking of a cohesive top team. Much of it is not even strategically significant.

Some of the thorniest issues in setting strategy are these: What data are needed, what information is relevant, what judgments can be made—and how will we combine the power of these to draw implications for the future of our business? Done properly, this work is the prelude to formulating a robust strategic vision.

Data, even when sifted and analyzed to yield useful information, are not enough in and of themselves. It has become clear that, for example, prior to the attacks of September 11, data about terrorists and their activities were not necessarily in short supply. Even the distillation of that data into more meaningful information was taking place. What was missing were the judgments that might have been made about the relative likelihood of certain kinds of attacks—and the implications (not to mention the preventive actions) that might have been drawn from those judgments.

Sadly, the world has learned once and for all that there are simply no "data" about the future. By their very nature, data are about the past and the present. When it comes to the future, where our strategic vision is to be implemented, there are only judgments to be made. Without moving from data to useful information, to assumptions based on that information, to judgments about the most likely scenarios, organizations will have little solid ground on which to base their strategic choices.

Organizations today face another kind of challenge. The plethora of raw data that can be made instantly available threatens to overwhelm any company's best thinkers. Although the knowledge management fad of the late 1990s helped some organizations with tracking problems and other operational statistics, we believe it did little to enhance judgment at the strategic level. More than ever, strategic teams must be disciplined in their focus on the data and information that are relevant to their critical choices—not simply the data that are easiest to obtain or are favorable to a given point of view.

That also means the team must meet head on the prima facie assumptions and predictions about the future that are passed off as truisms but that may in fact be based on arcane or dated information. With good judgment at the center, the work of strategic intelligence is more relevant than ever.

ASKING THE RIGHT QUESTIONS

The key to assessing data, agreeing on assumptions, and making judgments lies in asking the right questions. These central—and relatively few—questions have several things in common. They seek to explain the past and present, but they look to the future. They are not fundamentally about the financials. And they are universal. Although we tailor these questions slightly for our clients, there isn't one that needn't be considered in laying the groundwork for a well-crafted strategic vision. Yet there is nothing new or revolutionary about the territory they cover.

The World Around Us: Considering the Future

The first set of questions looks at broad areas of the external environment, largely outside the control of the organization, which will influence its potential for successful strategy.

- What are the key *economic trends* that could affect our nature or direction?
- What are the most significant *trends in society* for our business?
- What are the most significant and relevant *trends in government, politics, and legislation*?
- What major *technological trends* could affect our future?

The self-evident nature of these questions does not diminish their importance. They are deliberately far-reaching, rather than specific. Questions focused on micro-data only draw attention away from the relevance of the big picture.

When the data seem insufficient, team members should remember the motivation behind gathering data. Ultimately, the team needs sufficient data to draw out the implications of trends and assumptions *for its own business*. If the implications are not clear, the data may not be good enough. Otherwise, a certain amount of judgment is called for; and teams must be careful to avoid analysis paralysis.

For example, during this first phase of strategy, one team attempted to predict the precise level of interest rates for each quarter over the next 5 years. Their best answers, though not likely to be totally accurate, might have been important for setting strategy in the banking industry. But this company was a piping and tubing manufacturer. What's more, the top team anticipated a relatively low debt burden. They were trapped in micro-data that were ultimately irrelevant.

Occasionally, in-house expertise is called for. When executives on Keith Alm's team at Hallmark International were considering the potential market for "c-greetings" (greetings delivered via cell phones), they called in members of a tiny in-house group interested in digital greeting applications. The group was able to verify the validity of technological trends that supported a vision where c-greetings would find a potential market. (As Alm's team moved further along in the strategy process, however, they revisited the feasibility of this powerful new set of products and markets. They asked the larger Hallmark organization to fund further inquiry. Within months, the group received startup capital and has since been launched as an innovative subsidiary.)

The second set of externally focused questions helps the team identify the key players in the organization's current value chain and the trends that are likely to affect their behavior in the market. These questions include the following:

- Who are the major *customers*, *purchasers*, and *end users* of our products and/or services? How will the profiles of these groups likely evolve over the strategic time frame?
- What trends are likely in our *supplier* base?
- What significant developments do we expect in the overall *competitive scenario* and in the structure of our industry's *value chain*? What should we expect from our direct and indirect competitors, from new competitors, or from entirely new forms of competition?
- What are the *essential requirements for success* for any organization in our industry sector? How does our organization measure up against these requirements, compared with our competitors? Projecting our current capabilities into the future, what will be our unique strengths and critical vulnerabilities?

A client once asked if these data might be questionable since using the data seemed to require the team to make an assumption that its current position in the value chain would remain unchanged. Our answer was that any organization formulating its strategy should be open to this question. Roughly half of our clients see no significant value chain shifts as a result of the strategy engagement; one-quarter see major shifts in their emphasis on certain products, markets, or capabilities, and another quarter reassess their role so significantly that their central purpose is redefined.

Again, the focus must be on the information that is most likely to have a significant effect. The strategy team's first pass typically yields generic results. Its thinking on the requirements for success is likely to generate platitudes about quality or customer service. But after several iterations, more specific—and therefore powerful—distinctions emerge. The secret is in finding a balance between detailed information and analysis that may have some meaning in the broader picture.

For example, questions and judgments about the nature of future competitive threats have long dominated strategic discussions. Yet it is unlikely that specific information about one competitor's new market entries for a specific product line, or a move of all its manufacturing facilities to Asia, will affect your team's choices at a strategic level. Rather, it makes sense to understand one's major competitors at the strategic level—that is, what choices are our major competitors likely to make on the nine key components of a strategic vision? Teams should do this very instructive exercise for their two or three most likely *future* competitors. And in thinking through the implications of a competitor's choices, a company's own strategy may be brought into sharper focus.

In terms of customer trends, Alfred Chan's forced kitchen duty was part of his drive to focus on uniquely relevant information. "Starting then," Chan says, "the team began to realize that cooking is big business for us." A strong customer relationship continues to be the cornerstone of the Towngas strategy. In retrospect, Chan feels that "the most important thing was to get the top team to talk to our customers, become acquainted with our customer base, and understand our products in light of customer needs."

It was this kind of information that Keith Alm also insisted on for his strategy team. At Hallmark International, this meant close examination, even outright rejection, of assumptions about the value chain that had been borrowed from Hallmark in the United States. After an initial catch-up period of targeted market research, the team found that consumers around the world simply purchase and use "greetings" differently from consumers in the United States. Alm went one step further and instituted ongoing monitoring of local consumer trends that will ensure a solid understanding of Hallmark customers into the future.

For the consumable industrial tooling giant Kennametal, supplier data are the most critical. Kennametal's core products are built around tungsten, a naturally occurring but relatively rare material. Kennametal purchases tungsten both as ore and as a refined product. The solidity of its supplier relationships is crucial. When Jim Breisinger led the strategy team for Kennametal's newly consolidated Advanced Materials Solutions group, they carefully considered trends among Chinese producers of the ore, who control about 70 percent of the tungsten reserves worldwide. Even though Kennametal was not directly dependent on Chinese ore, their producers have a profound impact on its world price.

The key for every organization is the clarity about *which* information is critical. Reams of data about every imaginable trend are more likely to cloud the issue rather than help a team agree on how the external environment will affect the business.

The Internal Environment: Searching for Clues

Selective information about the past and present, however, can generate significant insights that help companies make strategic choices. Any existing organization has left in its trail a set of footprints that provide valuable clues for the future.

When such information about previous endeavors and experiences is analyzed effectively, it can help teams form common assumptions that will influence future success. For example, the following questions have proven their value many times over:

- What are examples of our *products and/or services* that have been clearly successful or unsuccessful in the past? What factors account for the difference?
- Which relationships with *customers or end users* have been particularly successful or unsuccessful? What factors account for the difference?
- What accounts for our previous successes or failures in various *geographic markets*?

Using a hierarchy of questions helps. First, identify clearly successful and unsuccessful examples. In each case, then understand the root cause of the success or failure. Identify the common elements in those causes to create organizational learning from the repeated, perhaps predictable, errors or successes of the past. Ask which of the elements were actually consciously deployed by the organization to create success. Finally, determine what conclusions can be made about future success.

Questions related to the internal dimensions of the strategy process are also important. Often, a careful probing of the answers reveals long-held assumptions that may or may not be true in the future.

- What *basic beliefs or values* affect the culture of our organization and influence or guide our strategic behavior?
- What is our *strategic history*? How have we categorized our products, services, and markets? Which products have we not offered, and why? Which markets have we not served, and why? What has been our competitive advantage?
- What *expectations*, if any, will the following have: parent company, shareholders, employees, customers, local communities, and unions?
- What are our measurements and expectations for *growth and return*? How do these compare with others in our industry?
- How well have we *implemented* previous strategies? What information supports our conclusions?
- Have our *business plans and annual budgets* accurately reflected our strategy, and if not, why?
- Do our *review processes* focus mainly on operational and financial results rather than on our strategy?

A company's strategic history can be especially revealing at this stage. Top teams may discover that their organizations have not been following one consistent direction, which will explain many of their current struggles. Even if the strategic focus has been clear in the past, much of its implementation may have been left undone. If those responsible for strategy have been undisciplined; if projects have not been delivered on time, to cost, and to specification; if strategy has not been regularly reviewed, updated, and communicated; if strategy has not been linked to the way the company manages its people; then, this information will inform decision making and foster the discipline needed to implement strategy in the future. The history of success in implementing strategy provides guidance to the current vision as well as its realization; past strategies may have been unrealistic, or based on environmental assumptions that proved to be false.

The answers to these final questions lead the top team into the next phase of strategy—namely, to craft the strategic vision itself. You will see how the results of a careful assessment can affect the quality of this vision in the next three chapters on strategy formulation.

GATHERING AND ANALYZING STRATEGIC INTELLIGENCE

The questions discussed above frame the gathering of strategically relevant data. Yet the top team has its hardest work ahead. The task in this phase is to use the data collected to move along the continuum from information, to judgment, to strategic insight and wisdom. The end product is a set of commonly held assumptions about both the external and internal environments in which the company will operate over its strategic time frame, and most importantly, their implications.

Often, more time is required to complete this phase than many executives would suspect. This is not always because the information is unavailable but because members of the top team simply have differing perceptions about the environment and individual biases in interpreting it. Similarly, they have different views of the causal factors for successes or failures. Some team members will always want more financial or marketing information than others. The team needs to navigate its way through this potential minefield to ensure its focus on the vital few questions.

Even at this early stage in the process, the CEO will need to lead his or her team decisively, make the call on how much information is enough, and shape the team's thinking so that it remains focused on the strategic dimensions of its environment.

This requires the following activities:

- *Gather accurate data:* Focus on the answers to the "vital few" strategically relevant questions. A primary source is the polling of strategy team members. For additional data gathering, the emphasis is on appropriate involvement of experts in the organization, as well as choosing the correct external sources. Research for its own sake should be avoided.

- *Distill data into a manageable quantity:* Identify common themes and issues for the top team to address. The team then creates a summary that reflects the group's best insights and sidesteps data overload. One rule of thumb: If a concern is not expressed by a majority of the group, it may not be strategically relevant. Yet there should always be room for the contrarian whose persuasive arguments can offer the group a real breakthrough.

- *Analyze and agree:* The team should now analyze and agree on the meaning of the information presented. They draft a set of assumptions, or agreed-to knowledge, that will guide its thinking from this point onward. Although difficult, it is often at the end of this stage that the team begins to sense that ownership by the whole will strengthen the strategy.

- *Judge*: Based on the environmental assumptions and implications, team members apply their best judgment to analyze potential problems and opportunities, to engage in what-if scenarios, to anticipate the future, and to foresee their organization's role in it.

    One distinction should be made at this point. The move from assumptions to implications is the difference between general knowledge and insight into the impact it has on the organization and its future strategic choices. A consumer products team agreed on the *assumption* that interest rates would remain at then-current levels. The *implication* for their business was that consumer spending would continue to grow in their industry sector, fueled by real income growth and unhampered by increased interest payments on mortgages and other debts. When implications are drawn, the team begins to paint the picture of how an organization should *respond* to environmental conditions. In other words, they make a set of judgments about the "shoulds" of the future.

- *Evaluate*: Before moving on to begin formulating the strategy itself, there must be a rigorous review of the validity of assumptions and implications. Where serious differences persist, the sources of information can be evaluated. If additional research can validate the team's thinking, it is undertaken. Academics, think-tank experts, and government models may all be consulted. Where gaps in information cannot be filled, or the implications drawn are less clear, the team must proceed with caution. In the final analysis, courage is needed, for the future is always unknowable.

If members of the strategy team don't inherently understand their business, they will find this journey an arduous one.

Several years ago, the top team of a global consumer products company demonstrated a remarkably weak collective understanding of the business. Among 11 participants, a laundry list of 30 direct competitors was generated—but only 9 of those were agreed on by more than 2 team members. Widespread confusion on the delineation of customers and end users made it nearly impossible to identify significant trends. And, sadly, when asked about the *unique* strengths of their organization, the team members had a list of 14—and of these 14, only 1 was agreed on by more than 2 participants! They did describe, however, 31 critical vulnerabilities—but again, only a handful were agreed to by more than 3 team members.

When these individuals were challenged to agree on environmental assumptions, they were paralyzed. Only after considerable time invested in catching up on their business fundamentals were they able to proceed.

The capacity of each team member for strategic thinking plays a pivotal role. The quality of the end result depends on his or her willingness to follow a disciplined process, as well as to engage in creative scenario building and self-effacing acceptance of other views. The chief executive who has carefully chosen the team members will reap the rewards for having done so.

 ## SEVEN MUSTS FOR TOP TEAMS

Inevitably, top teams vary widely in their strategic sophistication and the quality and content of their discussions. Yet every team moves most effectively through the process when its chief executive insists on these ground rules:

- Find the right answers through asking the right questions. By sticking to the central questions, each key piece of the strategic territory will eventually be covered.
- Continually zero in on the implications of the information for your own firm.
- Build a framework of trust. Avoid blindsiding the team with closely guarded data or a clever spin that seeks to score points rather than advance the group's thinking.
- Work hard to find common ground. Remember that areas of agreement are often powerful indicators of importance and relevance. Flexibility and compromise are always in order.
- Remain open to challenge. The naïve question or unique perspective of the outsider is often the true test of an assumption's validity.
- Take risks, and trust your own and others' judgment. Remember that none of you can predict the future; together, you will do your best to anticipate it.
- Trust the process. Setting strategy deserves the discipline you would accord any other crucial business process, combined with your most inspired creativity.

In the words of a chief executive who led his brilliant but stubborn team through this process, "It's damned hard work—harder than I ever imagined. Yet it's also the most efficient, rapid way I know of to bring a team together for the work that lies ahead."

IMPLICATIONS FOR THE STRATEGY PROCESS

The entire strategy process is intentionally iterative, and we expect that the strategic intelligence gathered in this phase will be revisited often. Nonetheless, the quality of the groundwork done here will have a profound effect on each of the remaining four phases of strategy formulation and implementation.

First, as you will see in the next three chapters, it will be the basis for constructing the strategic profile itself. These judgments are one source of the criteria against which strategic alternatives will be weighed. They will inform the organization's choices about its future nature and direction.

When it comes to the construction of the strategic profile, no set of judgments is foolproof. An exceptional case was that of a national postal service roughly a decade ago. When the top team agreed that the organization's competitive advantage lay in creating superior methods of distribution, it failed to anticipate how technology would radically transform the delivery of information, text, and materials. Perhaps the emergence of the Internet and our now-ubiquitous e-mail was simply unknowable. Perhaps the team should have dug more deeply into the technological frontiers, cross-examining technology visionaries about their intent. Perhaps they could have strengthened their strategy by fleshing out what-if scenarios—in this case, what if we're wrong?

Crown Greetings Ltd., the startup cell phone greeting division of Hallmark Cards, Inc., has joined the cluster of businesses frustrated by the delayed development of 3G technology in mobile phones. Crown's initial forecasts of mobile phone usage, the demand for mobile Internet access, and the introduction of technology to support mobile video streaming have had to be adjusted as advances in the industry have shifted to a slower pace.

The quality of strategic intelligence also profoundly affects an organization's approach to the activities of phases 3 and 4, Strategic Master Project Planning and Implementation. Insights gained by the top team, particularly those derived from assessing characteristics of the internal strategic environment, will invariably unearth valuable clues to guide implementation. For example, projects may be planned to fill the gaps in competitive or market research that are discovered. When the top team has honestly assessed the organization's strengths, weaknesses, and critical vulnerabilities, potential pitfalls along the implementation path are more easily avoided.

Finally, the team's assumptions will be key to monitoring the relevance of the organization's strategy over time. With important indicators already identified, tracking of trends and developments can be accomplished more systematically. And when major shifts are detected, the organization is ready to reassess its strategy and make the adjustments needed.

An extreme example of this came during the strategy work of Kennametal Europe. It was in the middle of the environmental assessment and analysis when Jim Breisinger determined that his European division would be able to acquire their major—and much larger—German competitor, Hertel. In short, the team's assumptions required radical reassessment before a strategy was even formulated.

Breisinger says that "the strategy process was very successful in integrating Hertel, which was the most successful acquisition Kennametal had ever had, and probably the largest value-creating activity in the organization during the 1990s." Rather than force his team's conclusions on Hertel's leaders, he literally started over to include reconsideration of a now-revised competitive scenario, as well as the views of Hertel's top team on external and internal assumptions and basic beliefs, to create a truly common and integrated set of insights.

We will revisit the importance of monitoring the strategy for its continuing viability in Chapter 12. In the meantime in the following chapter, however, we'll address the next step: establishing initial parameters for crafting the strategic profile.

4

Strategy Formulation: The Initial Parameters

At a leading financial services company in the United Kingdom, many team members suggested that their strategic time frame should be 5 to 6 years. Their CEO challenged them to reduce that to 4 years. His rationale was that the organization's internal clock was simply too slow and that its traditional approach to setting goals allowed for too leisurely a pace. External factors now demanded a speedier response.

When this team examined its basic beliefs, it identified a general slowness and resistance to innovation as a problem area. Since then, the team has formulated a basic belief that says the company will "set the pace in our marketplace to stay ahead of our competitors, especially in product innovation and addressing consumer trends."

This example highlights the two initial parameters—the strategic time frame and the organization's basic beliefs—that make up the starting point for strategy formulation, the second phase of our model. This chapter focuses on these parameters within which the strategic vision will be developed.

In the next two chapters we will continue our discussion of the strategy formulation phase. Chapter 5 is devoted to the concept of *Driving Force*. This powerful unifying principle is the key to identifying an organization's competitive advantage and to resolving major product and market choices and the decisions that flow from them. We also examine the concept of *key capabilities*.

In Chapter 6 we discuss the final components of the strategic vision that set the stage for implementation: the appropriate emphases and mix of products and markets that will drive an organization forward and its expectations for financial growth and return.

The core issue throughout the strategy formulation phase is whether a company's existing emphasis and mix of products, markets, and capabilities form a winning combination for the future. The challenge lies in reponding to these questions: Why are you in the business you are in and not another? Why do you offer the products you do and serve the markets you are in, and not others? What exactly is your organization about?

The answers to these questions help a team draw the line between what's in and what's out, and they provide guidance for handling the gray areas in between. They also help a strategy team unravel these remaining issues:

- What are the basic beliefs and values that guide our organization?
- What is our major source of competitive advantage? How will we strengthen and develop that advantage?
- What key capabilities do we need to take our products to market?
- How will we allocate scarce resources effectively, based on a rational portfolio of priorities?
- What will be our direction and scope for growth and new business? From which incompatible, noncore, or unprofitable products, services, and markets should we retreat?
- What are our underlying expectations for return and profit?

When the strategic vision is complete, it is the roadmap for strategy implementation, helping to:

- Provide input on organization structure and staffing decisions
- Give a common theme to internal communications and their clarity
- Provide direction for external marketing, advertising, and public relations

- Provide guidance for operational and day-to-day decision making
- Create a unity of purpose and common culture in the organization
- Create a human performance system that incorporates rewards and consequences to support strategic behaviors
- Act as a source of guidelines for business planning

THE STRATEGIC TIME FRAME

The most basic parameter of a strategic vision is its time frame. Like any other goal or project, a strategic profile must describe an endpoint. Otherwise, there is no sense of urgency or constraint associated with strategy implementation. Progress will either be slower than expected or driven artificially by calendar months or planning and budgeting cycles. A defined time frame, no matter how long, focuses the development of environmental assumptions. Later, it is the foundation for sequencing and coordinating implementation across divisions, functions, and geographical areas. More importantly, it is the axis for measurement of organizational and employee performance against strategic objectives.

The strategic time frame varies dramatically among organizations. Its length reflects the value chain in which an organization participates, its unique internal characteristics, and the external variables that impact its domain.

If the time frame is too short, it will not allow for the full realization of strategic ambitions. If it is too long, the team may struggle to make its vision concrete and actionable.

Ask yourself about the forces that affect your own company's sense of strategic time. How do shifts in the world at large—the rate of macroeconomic change, the amount and accessibility of information, emerging legal and regulatory constraints—affect your enterprise? What is the overall rate of change in your industry? What is the impact of relevant market trends, technological developments, shifts in demographic patterns, and emerging competitive threats? Within your company, what is the receptivity to change? What general pace has characterized your best efforts? How long is the typical product development cycle? Are there large operational projects that will affect your timing in implementing strategy? The answers to these questions confirm that any company's strategic time frame is uniquely its own.

A strategic time frame is emphatically *not* the same as the time period for long-range planning activities. Typically, long-range planning reflects specified intervals to comply with accounting and shareholder expectations. Planning horizons are often arbitrary. At Hertz Rent A Car in the early 1970s, thinking about the future was dominated by the need to do annual budgets and 3-year long-range plans; there was no logic to the 3-year time frame.

At Xerox, planning was the consuming passion; there were 1-year budgets, product plans, market plans, and financial plans, and all were complements to a 7-year long-range plan. But sadly, the obsession with planning minutiae obscured the strategic big picture. Xerox did not look beyond its various planning cycles to strategic time, and it therefore failed to act on intelligence about Japanese competition. The rest is history.

The only correct strategic time frame is the one that works for your company. The Consumer Products Division of Courtaulds Textiles, which designed and manufactured clothing for retailers, adopted a strategic time frame of 1 to 2 years. Rapid shifts in both fashions and fabrics would have made any longer-ranging assumptions invalid. In contrast, the Bord Na Mona in Ireland (the state peat bog board) set a 20-year strategic horizon. This parameter reflected the time required to change land-use patterns; this was necessary as the peat was depleted and new farming and recreation uses were planned.

An even more dramatic example is that of a half-billion-dollar privately held U.S. conglomerate. This company is owned by family trusts that control its equity and dividend distributions and make all decisions on investments, acquisitions, and disposals. Because these trusts exist to assure not only the interests of the current generation but those of their children as well, they have appropriately established a 30-year strategic time frame.

We need to be realistic about the usefulness of the strategic time frame in practice. The world around us does not respect artificial time boundaries, nor does it necessarily march forward at a single pace. As the preceding examples demonstrate, organizations must adopt a time frame that is in step with its industry's dynamics.

Business leaders have long observed, particularly when undergoing major change, that progress is measured in two steps forward, one step back. No matter how carefully we plan or anticipate, progress is never linear; inevitably, there are unanticipated factors that interrupt our forward motion. Think of the results of the current genome project: It has revolutionized the entire biotechnology industry. Then there is the Internet. Nearly every industry has been affected by the connectivity the Internet affords and the e-business opportunities it has created. Anticipated time frames have simply collapsed with electronic speed. Our observations tell us what our intellects find hard to accept: The theoretical physicists are right, and time is indeed relative.

Let's say we're in the pharmaceutical industry, in a company that prides itself on being first to market with innovative products. We've found the cure for the common cold, and according to our internal project management clock, we'll take it to market right on schedule. But the world around us does not respect our time lines. If a competitor beats us to market, our product will hit the shelves as an alternative, not a breakthrough. Our company's position is always relative, and our sense of being out in front may be out of tune with others' reality.

Pragmatically, we insist that the strategy team establish a time frame when it begins the strategy formulation phase. Most teams should bear in mind that today's strategic ambitions will need to be informed by the acceleration of time frames in the years and decades to come.

Naturally, the time frame itself is subject to review and modification as the process goes forward. Its primary purpose is to provide a parameter for strategic deliberations and a reference point for measuring implementation progress. Every top team will also work with tools intended to compensate for the discontinuity between their internal clocks and external reality: analysis of potential problems and opportunities, sophisticated project management frameworks, what-if models, and techniques for forecasting and scenario building.

Best-practice imperatives demand that strategy be kept "evergreen." When a robust approach to monitoring, reviewing, and updating the strategy is in place, its formulation and implementation must be a never-ending and dynamic process. But, for example, a time frame indicating that "by the year 2005, we will have . . ." helps teams make their visioning concrete.

THE ROLE OF BASIC BELIEFS

In 1999 the author was invited by the president of the Oxford University Union to lead a debate on the motion, "This House believes that profit should come before principles." The side he led opposed the motion. It included the chairman of Shell U.K. and a Trotskyist (a rare breed these days). The Shell group had just emerged from a series of environmental and human rights crises and had, in response, gone through a searching exercise to re-evaluate its own beliefs and values. The opposing view was represented by the World Debating Champion, the head of a right-wing thinktank, and the deputy editor of The Economist.

Our argument that there should be overriding beliefs and values that have a very strong influence on the nature, direction, and behavior of corporations and that transcend the profit motive won the day.

Today's corporations face increasing pressure to examine and act on a set of values and beliefs. The continuing demonstrations against the World Trade Organization and the International Monetary Fund are part of a mindset that asks companies to rebalance their priorities. So too are the horrified reactions of millions of employees and investors to the accounting scandals exposed in mid-2002.

We define a basic belief as a deeply held tenet, creed, conviction, or persuasion. It is one that speaks to the intrinsic and/or tangible value of a human or material condition. Basic beliefs provide the social cohesion of organizations. They give to an organization a sense of meaning that transcends the sell-more–spend-less creed that defines almost all business transactions.

However, many organizations have basic beliefs or value statements that are little more than corporate pieties. In other organizations, basic beliefs and values are not explicitly stated. They remain a hidden influence and are never put on the table for discussion, evaluation, or change. Without closely examining these "invisible" beliefs—clarifying, recrafting (when needed), or even casting them out—organizations run the risk of having such beliefs adversely affect decision making and behaviors.

What's more, basic beliefs are an important aspect of strategy implementation. They set boundaries for day-to-day decision making, provide a sense of cohesion that reinforces strategic unity, and support desired performance by setting a standard for accountability. Clearly formulated basic beliefs that are visible to all stakeholders in an organization, relevant to decision making, and useful in guiding and testing behaviors are an immensely powerful tool.

That's why we insist that a strategy team must discuss and codify its basic beliefs right up front. They are first considered during the strategic intelligence phase, and they become an important touchstone throughout as the team formulates and audits the remaining components of its vision.

Where Do Basic Beliefs Come From?

Most executives instinctively understand the nature of basic beliefs and probably can articulate the beliefs they and their companies currently hold (either by choice or default). Less obvious is the origin of those beliefs and their alignment with the other components of strategic intent. In articulating the basic beliefs of your strategy, consider the following questions:

What were the basic beliefs of the founders of our company? How have they been articulated and demonstrated? In many instances, beliefs and values stem from the founders of an organization. At our own firm, Kepner-Tregoe, this is certainly the case. Three of our basic beliefs have been with us since the company began more than 40 years ago.

The first of these expresses a commitment to the power of process in managing organizations. It states that we will "build upon our worldwide leadership in *process* facilitation, consulting, and skill development." Kepner-Tregoe will never be a firm of content consultants, and this is what our founders intended.

Second, we state that we will "*transfer* our ideas to clients, enabling them to do for themselves rather than having us do for them." It expresses the old Chinese proverb that "it is better to teach a man to fish so that he may feed himself for life than to give him a fish so he can eat for a day."

Third, we will "produce practical, useful *results* for our clients." We stand or fall by the true value added that we provide. These three basic beliefs are so ingrained into the Kepner-Tregoe culture that the code words *process, transfer,* and *results* are immediately recognized by employees and clients alike, and they govern our daily activities.

What other beliefs have evolved in the organization and been accepted over time? How have they been implemented and accepted, formally or informally? How do they govern our decision making, people management, and day-to-day behavior? Recognizing the beliefs and values that have emerged in the company is vital to predicting those that will shape its future. Of course, this cuts both ways. It is just as important to recognize—and jettison—beliefs that are irrelevant, perhaps damaging, or not aligned with the strategic intent. Indeed, some beliefs may be held only by certain groups, which is often a source of conflict.

In a classic case of the need to "deprogram" certain beliefs, there was the young CEO who had inherited the reins of a $700 million privately held firm upon the death of his father. Three years later, the son still found himself asking "what would my father do" at every turn. To make way for a new strategic vision, he had to closely examine—and give up—several of his father's long-held but restricting beliefs in order to define beliefs of his own. For example, he now believes that his father's autocratic style of management is no longer appropriate and that a more participatory leadership style will yield better results.

In which areas of the organization—our processes, our products, our performance, our marketplace, our capabilities—do we aspire to leadership? How do we express these things to others (internally and externally)? What differentiates our company in the minds of all our stakeholders? Basic beliefs are at the heart of a strategy. At Kepner-Tregoe, for example, leadership in process-oriented services and their application through facilitation is at the core of our being.

One firm states that it will offer only products that are "in demonstrable, proven, profitable, niche technologies that we understand." One of the company's niches is metal tubing with highly specialized technical requirements. Every one of its products in this category—whether made for medical equipment, aircraft, or oil refineries—ranks first, second, or third in market share. This and several other niches are what management understands, and they reject ventures into other product areas, no matter how attractive.

What qualities in our people are central to exploiting our key capabilities? Ideally, what is the relationship between our company and our employees? What intangible qualities do we promote when recruiting new people for the organization? At their best, how do our people behave with each other? Another of our own basic beliefs says that we will "work for the greater good of the Kepner-Tregoe family worldwide while valuing individual needs." Our firm is global in scope, with everyone frequently on the move and often working in small teams. This basic belief gives us a steady compass point for employee relationships, strengthening our overall cohesion as a company.

What is the nature of our relationship with our stakeholders (for example, with our board, parent, subsidiaries, shareholders, partners, and local communities)? What expectations do they have for our behavior? There are many firms whose ethical and moral beliefs about business practices constrain them from marketing to, sourcing from, or cooperating with countries whose customs and practices do not conform to their own. Similarly, other companies are at long last under both internal and external pressure to review certain practices—in relation to child labor, the export of produce that does not conform to European Union standards, and potential violation of international environmental treaties.

At Towngas, the strategy team examined the specific outcomes it wanted to achieve with each of its identified stakeholder groups: customers, shareholders, employees, and the community in which it operates. As it moves into new locations in China, for example, natural gas will not be made available to households with substandard delivery systems until the systems are upgraded. The Towngas basic belief regarding customer safety will not permit a compromise on this count.

An even simpler example: The Bristol and West Bank has been headquartered in Bristol since its inception. Despite the many benefits that might accrue with a move to the United Kingdom's financial center in London, its relationship with the Bristol community is such that remaining there, it believes, is in the best interests of all its constituents.

Stakeholders may influence not only the content of an organization's beliefs and values but their implementation as well. At a major airline, a framework of beliefs about employees and work practices was developed in cooperation with its many trade unions—a process that helped to turn a hostile and adversarial relationship into one that was both positive and instrumental in implementing those beliefs.

Characteristics of Basic Beliefs

Basic beliefs are about stuff, not fluff. Statements like "We value our employees," or "The customer is king," or "Quality is Job 1" may make decent advertising copy, but they don't have the strategic depth that makes a difference.

To be strategically useful, an organization's basic beliefs must be:

- *Universal*: Basic beliefs apply to every level of the organization, to every employee, every function, and every location, with no exceptions. Where appropriate, they apply to external constituencies as well.
- *Realistic*: Although no organization is perfect, its basic beliefs should express attainable goals for continuous implementation.
- *Clearly stated and easily understood*: If a basic belief is ambiguous or couched in jargon, it is meaningless. Every employee should be able to grasp the intent of each basic belief, as should any other constituent to whom it is relevant.
- *Measurable*: A basic belief should identify distinctly the kinds of observable behaviors and standards that will be used to assess how well employees and the organization as a whole measure up.
- *Demonstrable*: Everyone should be able to see the basic beliefs "in action." Role modeling by top managers is especially crucial; without it they will rightly be accused of producing a package that *is* all pomp and no circumstance.
- *Consequential*: Quite simply, if a company's basic beliefs have no impact on its decision making, they are irrelevant. Basic beliefs are a powerful strategic unifier only when they are owned and implemented throughout the organization.

Most companies settle on a relatively few basic beliefs, usually between 8 and 12. They frequently have strategic, operational, and human dimensions.

When we worked with the J.M. Smucker Company, its basic beliefs were focused on five key words: *quality*, *ethics*, *independence*, *growth*, and

people. This family-owned American icon in the jams and jellies category exemplifies the power of basic beliefs in strategic thinking. Consider
their statement on quality; it addresses both strategic and operational
issues, speaks to the relationship with employees, customers, and stakeholders, and codifies values that establish what the company will and
will not pursue:

**Quality is the key word and shall apply to our people, our prod-
ucts, our manufacturing methods, and our marketing efforts. We
will market the highest-quality products offered in our respective
markets:**

- **Consistent high quality is required.**
- **The company's growth and success have been built on quality.**
- **Quality comes first; then earnings and sales growth will follow.
  We will only produce and sell products that enhance the qual-
  ity of life and well-being.**

Implementing Basic Beliefs

Tacking a basic beliefs plaque up on the wall will not suffice. Taking our
own medicine, at Kepner-Tregoe we work hard to communicate our
beliefs, recognizing and rewarding those individuals who exemplify
them. Adherence to basic beliefs is among the selection criteria for part-
nership and election to the board; as a criterion in annual performance
appraisals; for disciplinary purposes; and, in assessing the quality of
our client relationships and assignments through our customer surveys.

The beliefs are featured on posters and wallet-size cards at nearly
every desk. A basic beliefs committee is selected and chaired by the
company's founder. This group evaluates nominations for quarterly and
annual recognition. The process is keenly followed, and those employees who are singled out have their success celebrated throughout the
company.

We know that our basic beliefs are meaningless unless they result in
behaviors that support our strategy. We encourage client strategy
teams, at an early stage in the engagement, to consider how their basic
beliefs will be implemented and how success in achieving each belief
will be measured. For example, an organization aspiring to technologi-

cal leadership might examine and measure the number of patents registered each year relevant to its core products.

Nature abhors a vacuum, and without a set of commonly held basic beliefs, individuals will establish their own sense of purpose and values. The beliefs they choose may have a certain validity, but they will not be necessarily aligned with the strategy. However well-intended, individuals may be working at cross-purposes, and this will eventually drain resources and erode strategic unity.

Basic beliefs are not a nice-to-have; rather, they explain how an organization goes about its business. They are crucial to successful strategy implementation, aligning the organization's communications, culture, and practices with its strategic vision.

First, however, basic beliefs act as an important parameter for the remaining work of crafting the vision. The strategy team will use both these beliefs and the strategic time frame as fundamental stakes in the ground as they formulate their strategy.

5

Strategy Formulation: The Power of Driving Force

Late in the evening once after a long day's strategy session, my colleagues and I had a healthy argument about whether the strength of a certain organization was derived from its products or its customer relationships. We made a wager and decided to test the point—whether Harrods of London, the ultimate department store, would go to any length to meet a customer's request.

The next morning, we phoned Harrods and asked for the pet department. We were put through, and as expected, the magnanimous salesperson offered to help. "I'd like to order an elephant," said our colleague. "Certainly, sir," replied the Harrods employee. "Now, would that be an Asian elephant or an African elephant?"

DRIVING FORCE: ITS PURPOSE AND POWER

The phrase *Driving Force* has become common parlance over the last 20 years; however, it was first coined as a pivotal strategy concept by Kepner-Tregoe in the 1970s. For us, it provides the means of getting to the heart of any organization's strategic profile.

Driving Force is defined as "the *primary* determinant of the products and services an organization will and will not offer and the markets (customers, consumers, and geographies) it will and will not serve."[1] Over the past two decades, this definition has stood the test of time. It speaks concisely to the nature and direction of an organization, expressing the essence of "what our business is about."

Once an organization has established its basic beliefs and set its time frame, it is ready to create a set of alternative strategic visions for consideration. This is the crux of the strategy formulation process, and the Driving Force concept is the key.

The Driving Force provides focus, the basis for competitive advantage, guidance on the scope of products and markets, an indicator of "must-have" key capabilities, a communications vehicle, a means of unifying an organization, a source of decision-making criteria, and a means of evaluating competitors' strategies. The Driving Force also acts as a filter for new growth opportunities that appear and a guide for the phasing out of products and markets. It is a powerful tool for determining the fit of possible acquisitions, joint ventures, and alliances, as well as for guiding decision making when a predator proposes a takeover.

We have found that every organization has at its strategic core one of the following eight Driving Forces:

Products (or Services) Offered	Method of Sale (and/or Distribution)
Markets Served	Technology
Low-Cost Production	Natural Resources
Operations Capability	Return/Profit

Every organization we have worked with has found its Driving Force in one of these eight constructs—despite the occasional attempt by a client to invent a new Driving Force or redefine an existing one.

In some organizations, the current Driving Force is a forever concept. It remains the core of an organization's product and market choices. For example, it is quite likely that the U. S. Forest Service will continue to have a Natural Resources Driving Force. Bill Gates may claim that a Technology Driving Force will always guide Microsoft—though others could take issue with that view. And General Electric, the quintessential conglomerate, probably has the Return/Profit Driving Force at its core.

The comprehensive nature of the eight Driving Forces—and their easily distinguished implications for an organization's future—reflects the universality of the Driving Force construct. We have seen them applied in every conceivable type of concern, from governments to religious orders, in public- and private-sector firms, from single-plant manufacturers to multi-billion-dollar holding companies, across national boundaries and in widely disparate industries.

THE MOST COMMON DRIVING FORCES

Many of the organizations we work with, perhaps as many as half, select the Products (or Services) Offered Driving Force. The Markets Served Driving Force is also a more common choice than the remaining six alternatives. Since a mix of products and markets are at the heart of every company's strategy, it is only logical that these two are the most common.

The Return/Profit Driving Force has its own distinctive role in firms driven solely by financial parameters. Other Driving Forces, for example, Technology or Method of Distribution, focus an organization on the third element of the strategic equation—the organization's key capabilities for taking products to markets. The Driving Forces vary in character; therefore, they lead to entirely different portfolios of products and markets and sources of competitive advantage.

In some instances, to describe each of these, we give examples of well-known organizations that are not our clients. These are included for illustrative purposes only, and the reader should form his or her own judgment about the fit between these organizations and a given Driving Force.

We begin here with the two most common.

Products (or Services) Offered

A Products Offered organization meets a basic and enduring need in the marketplace by offering a limited range of products. The organization's core products will have significant synergy in meeting the basic need (for an automobile manufacturer that addresses the need for personal transport: cars, station wagons, and sports vehicles, for example).

Ancillary products and services are offered if, and only if, they further the sales of the core range (automobile manufacturers that provide loan financing, insurance, even clothing to promote the sale of their cars).

One of the most common dilemmas an organization faces is the choice between a narrowly focused and a more broadly focused Products Offered alternative. In a sense, these are different strategies. For example, a Products Offered *automobile* company might choose to venture into trucks, buses, and motorcycles. These vehicles serve a similar basic need—transportation—but more broadly defined. The company may remain Products Offered, but it is now in the business of *road transport*, not automobiles. Should trains, boats, and planes be added to the mix, it will become a *transport* company. Such evolutions are common; nevertheless, they must be undertaken with considerable strategic forethought.

A Products Offered organization will not include in its portfolio any products or services that have radically different end-use characteristics, or that meet completely new types of needs. If it does, it will need to alter the scope of its Products Offered Driving Force, or select a different Driving Force. In the next chapter, we examine more fully the relationship between the Driving Force concept and the thrust for new business.

Customers and end users of a Products Offered organization perceive its products or services as superior to (or unavailable from) its competitors. This differentiation is based on one or more characteristics: uniqueness, price, value, packaging, quality, or supporting benefits (such as warranties or service). As a result, the company will continually undertake product improvements, modifications, upgrades, and extensions of its product line. It will not venture into entirely new products that meet a very different need.

A Products Offered organization seeks to penetrate current demographic, geographic, or industrial markets as fully as possible before pursuing growth through the extension of markets or the creation of entirely new markets. For this reason, it needs to be fully attuned to its customers' buying motives.

The competitive advantage of a Products Offered firm is derived from its product differentiation, which lies in both the real benefits delivered and in end-user perceptions. The company's product differentiation must be both distinctive and superior to its competitors in order to maintain or increase market share.

The key capabilities a Products Offered organization exploits to sustain competitive advantage are most often related to product research, product development, sales, and distribution, as well as research on its customers and the marketplace.

Examples of Products Offered companies include Rolex, Toys R' Us, and I.C.I. Paints. Each has a narrow product range that meets an enduring, well-defined need. Though these companies produce and sell hundreds of items, they are distinguished by what they offer: watches, toys, paints.

Markets Served

While a Products Offered organization provides a limited range of products to an unlimited marketplace, a Markets Served organization does just the opposite. These companies build a powerful relationship, or franchise, with a clearly defined and often narrow group of customers or consumers who have common characteristics. This type of enterprise will produce (or acquire) products that meet a variety of its market's basic needs, since its synergy lies in its consumer base and its characteristics.

A Markets Served company pursues growth and new business through offering an ever-increasing number of products to its chosen marketplace. It will not venture into entirely new marketplaces that have characteristics that differ from the core market. It understands and supports its customers' buying patterns, psychology, range of needs, and sense of loyalty.

The competitive advantage that a Markets Served enterprise enjoys is achieved through sustaining a superior relationship with its chosen market and fulfilling its needs better than its rivals. When it succeeds, it generates fierce customer loyalty, and company and brand identification. Image and reputation for such a company are vital. The customer's perception of the organization is as important as the products themselves or their price/value relationship.

Such franchises are hard to come by, yet extremely compelling. Just try convincing a teenager (or an adult, for that matter) to change from Nike shoes and clothing to Reebok. The key capabilities of a Markets Served company focus on creating and maintaining this loyal customer base. Such a company actively assesses customers' needs through market research, and it seeks to match these ever-increasing needs with a wide range of products. Industry sectors where we often see Markets Served companies include luxury goods (e.g., Dunhill) and street fashions (e.g., Nike).

The United Kingdom–based retail giant Marks & Spencer is one firm that traditionally capitalized on the huge consumer loyalty of a chosen socioeconomic group. The chain subsequently diversified from clothing into food and flowers, and eventually into products ranging from greeting cards to financial services. Its subsequent purchase of the United States–based Brooks Brothers was less successful. Brooks Brothers' "preppy" customers had quite different characteristics from the well-established middle-class Marks & Spencer demographic. During the 1990s, Marks & Spencer began to lose touch with its traditional customers, failing to understand their shifting expectations. By the end of the decade, the company nearly folded—an awesome example of how to lose one's strategic way.

To summarize, a Markets Served organization offers a wider range of products to meet the expanding needs of its market franchise or customer group; its competitive advantage is rooted in the hold it has on the loyalties of its customers.

A Products Offered company seeks new business by moving into new marketplaces; a Markets Served organization looks first to new products for growth.

Because every company has products and markets, most will consider at least the Products Offered and Markets Served Driving Forces in their selection of a Driving Force. Each of the remaining six Driving Forces has its own distinctive traits that suggest a unique source of competitive advantage, the key capabilities required, a product/market scope, and a thrust for pursuing new business.

The Return/Profit Driving Force

Aren't we here to make money? Early on and without fail, often before we have been engaged by an organization, the chief executive or a top team member will fix on the Return/Profit Driving Force. At first blush, his or her point is obvious; without financial performance, all other choices are meaningless. We maintain, however, that meeting the financial goals of an organization—revenue and profit growth, improving margins and return on investment, a healthy balance sheet, and an ample cash flow—are the *result* of its strategic vision, rather than its primary raison d'être. For a Return/Profit-driven company, projected financial returns are the sole arbiters for choosing the product/market scope of a firm; in other firms, they take their place alongside other, more important criteria. Without this important distinction, every company might ultimately pursue an unbounded product/market portfolio, chasing every financial opportunity.

One top team tried to resolve its struggle with this by answering the following question: If your Driving Force were Return/Profit—with product and market decisions driven by maximizing financial gain—which product areas would you pursue? On the list generated, the team proposed exchanging its existing products for some very creative high-margin alternatives—computers, ice cream, and brothels among them. One participant finally failed to contain himself: "We can't get into brothels and ice cream!" he said. "We don't know anything about ice cream!"

With that remark, he had unwittingly made the point. If his had been a Return/Profit organization, the team wouldn't need to understand anything about ice cream or any other product area. The only salient factor would be performance on financial objectives. A true Return/Profit company would simply buy its way into any additional capabilities it needed.

Automobile industry icon Robert Lutz, now chairman of General Motors North America, has become known for his challenging "immutable laws of business." One of these is that "the primary purpose of business is not to make money."[2] Lutz says that focusing solely on the financials confuses the strategy of the business with the reward for achieving it. Under the pressure for short-term profits driven by analysts and stock markets, many companies have sacrificed strategic coherence for short-term expediency.

Following are brief descriptions of the six remaining Driving Forces. More detailed explanations of these appear in our earlier books on strategy.[3]

Other Driving Forces

Low-Cost Production

This type of organization offers a limited range of products; its superiority lies in offering a strong price/value relationship. Its focus is on the ability to produce goods more cheaply than its competitors. It derives competitive advantage from price as it passes on cost advantages to its customers. All its key capabilities are related to production processes, skills, and investment in equipment and related services. Examples of Low-Cost Production organizations include commodity companies and many firms in the steel industry.

Technology

A company pursuing this Driving Force builds its vision around a body of knowledge and/or a set of capabilities that enable it to develop new technologies or enhance existing ones. Its key capabilities are research and development. It supports innovation to satisfy existing and emerging needs or to create completely new needs. Its competitive advantage lies in the development, acquisition, and management of unique and superior technological expertise and its application to leading-edge products. It will seek as wide a range of markets for these as possible. Many young IT companies find that they set out with a Technology Driving Force. Examples of Technology driven may include Cisco and Goretex. Today's startup biotechnology companies are also likely to be Technology driven.

Natural Resources

This organization will own or control one or more of the world's significant natural resources. It may make usable products for direct sale to consumers, or it may sell its resources to intermediaries for use as raw materials. These companies' competitive advantage lies in the quality, quantity, location, form, and/or cost of exploitation of the natural resources themselves. Companies in the oil, natural gas, and forestry product sectors often have a Natural Resources Driving Force.

Method of Sale (and/or Distribution)

These similar Driving Forces act on their logistical, distribution, and sales capabilities, as well as the human and systems resources needed to exploit them fully. They provide a varying range of products and services within chosen marketplaces, and their sales or distribution channels may handle others' compatible products. Typical examples include express mail deliverers (Method of Distribution) and telemarketing or in-home sales organizations (Method of Sale).

Operations Capability

An organization pursuing an Operations Capability Driving Force has a set of capabilities—human and physical resources, systems, processes, flexibility, service levels, and a reputation for "getting things done"—that, used in a variety of combinations, produces a wide range of products or services. Such companies' competitive advantage lies in their superiority within a certain domain (for example, printing, metal fabricating, or trading). They offer a 24/7/365 one-stop solution on any scale, from a single customized piece to high-volume runs. Many companies that offer a turnkey solution for outsourcing IT capabilities, for example, may have an Operations Capability Driving Force. Copy shop chains and franchises come to mind in the copy and printing industry.

Return/Profit

As stated earlier, the Return/Profit–driven organization determines the scope of its portfolio based on specific levels of financial return and profit. An organization that seeks to improve its financial results and yet stay within its current product and market scope is not Return/Profit–driven. Rather, this Driving Force demands that financial targets determine its product and market choices. These are constrained only by the need to produce a minimum level of return and meet other financial hurdle rates related to cash and the cost of capital. Examples may include General Electric, Tyco, and Hanson.

Hallmark International: Avoiding the Obvious

At Hallmark International, Keith Alm's core leadership team dug deeper than most into the two most common alternatives, Products Offered and Markets Served. Confronted by several years of declining revenues, Alm and his team had no choice but to get clarity immediately. As they struggled to find a framework for cohesion among 18 business units around the globe, they also examined their U.S. counterpart more closely.

At face value, thought Alm, Hallmark's companies in the United States had to be Products Offered. Yet the team observed that, although the core line of cards and related products met the enduring need people have to express their thoughts and emotions, Hallmark's product lines in the United States had expanded dramatically to meet a much broader range of needs. The Hallmark Hall of Fame television broadcasts began in the 1950s, and Hallmark Entertainment is now the world's leading producer and distributor of miniseries and movies made for television. Hallmark owns Binney & Smith and their ubiquitous Crayola crayon product. In 1999 it acquired the Picture People, nationwide portrait studios housed primarily in shopping malls. Plush toys, ceramic collectibles, inspirational posters, home décor, and a plethora of other items populate its retail stores.

Alm's team saw that Hallmark in the United States had many characteristics of a Markets Served organization. Its clientele—overwhelmingly female, middle aged, middle income, middle of the road, with mainstream Midwestern values of family and personal connection—was discrete and clearly recognizable. In fact, it offered a broad array of products to meet the needs of consumers with these shared characteristics. In other words, its unstated Driving Force could easily fit the profile of a Markets Served company.

In the global arena of Hallmark International, however, there were already telling signs that a similar strategy would not succeed. The Plush category had never shown a profit, and the international market share in greeting cards had never matched that of the United States. Nowhere was there such a strong franchise. Only the United Kingdom had the scale potentially to support a diverse range of products, and the strain was showing there as well as in smaller markets, like those in Singapore and Hong Kong.

Hallmark International had repeatedly gravitated back to the North American norm—and it was killing them. A key factor, Alm believed, was that consumers in the international markets were poorly understood—and that they simply didn't share the attributes of their U.S. counterparts. Cultural behaviors and norms, holidays, religious observances, and relationships among family and friends all varied widely.

The team considered a Products Offered Driving Force. Hallmark International's strength (at least by default) lay in greeting cards and closely related products; it expected to meet the enduring needs of its customers for greetings, expressing care, and building relationships. Thus it decided to offer greeting products designed according to the consumer needs to be discovered through research rather than force fitting products that were successful in North America.

The team also considered the Method of Distribution Driving Force, based on the success of Hallmark's U.S. distribution network.

But, this strength would have been difficult for Hallmark International to replicate. The Operations Capability Driving Force also seemed a possibility, with its emphasis on creative product development and outstanding production capabilities.

After deliberating long and hard and receiving the initial results of market research, Hallmark International settled on the Products Offered Driving Force. It played to the entity's strengths.

The lessons learned by this team were instructive for many organizations. It managed to avoid the easy assumptions about Driving Force alternatives—the need for alignment with the U.S. parent and an aversion to ambiguity—that are made by many teams. The team saw the value of championing alternative strategic visions; it practiced the art of blue-sky thinking as well as the discipline of making tough choices in a rational way. It also grew in stature as intellectual rigor replaced the initial skepticism about the process. The valuable lessons learned from unchosen Driving Forces were to remain a source of inspiration throughout the rest of the process.

CHOOSING THE DRIVING FORCE

Selecting the optimum Driving Force is one of the most important and powerful decisions made by a leadership team. It demands an equally powerful process for making that choice.

Indeed, as demonstrated in Chapter 2, the application of a logical, visible, and rational sequence of steps in decision making helps a team avoid bias and the temptation to force fit a set of objectives against alternative scenarios, while allowing it to harness creativity to generate a variety of possible strategic profiles. This sequence is one of the key areas in the strategy process where art and discipline meld. Following is a brief description of how this works.

Effective strategic decision making begins with the creation of a set of objectives drawn from an organization's strategic intelligence. These are ranked by degrees of relative importance since they will not all be of equal weight. Next, a number of alternative future strategic visions, based on, perhaps, three or four different Driving Forces, are developed by members of the top team, championed, tested as far as possible, and further refined. When the alternative visions have been clearly articulated, they are communicated to the full group, and its understanding of each of them is tested. The team then evaluates each alternative rigorously against the criteria. If the superiority of a single alternative is not immediately clear, the two that have scored best are subjected to a disciplined risk assessment process before the final choice is made.[4]

The decision analysis for choosing a Driving Force often requires several days' work by the top team, as well as some off-site testing of the alternative visions. There is a considerable amount of both art and discipline required at this crucial stage of the strategy formulation process.

Zeroing In: How One Company Selected a Driving Force

Our work with a financial services organization demonstrates this decision process at work. This European banking institution had decided some years earlier to grow by diversifying beyond its historic savings-and-loan services. It had launched major forays into real estate, offshore banking, insurance, investment banking, and financial planning. The resulting lack of focus, inadequate investment available for building each product line, drain on executive time, and unclear operational priorities had caused it to drop from the top to the bottom quartile in industry rankings and to provide below-average returns to its investors. The company neglected its core business, dramatically increased its costs, and installed systems that were too convoluted for mere mortals to use.

The firm set out to reevaluate its strategy and to choose a Driving Force from the four that seemed most likely: Low-Cost Production Capability, Return/Profit, and Products Offered, both narrowly and broadly defined.

The team moved forward to establish its decision criteria and determine their relative importance. Some of these were as follows:

Criteria	Relative Weight (1–10, 10 = Highest)
Maximize our ability to outperform traditional and new competitors	10
Maximize our ability to create sustainable competitive advantage	10
Motivate our executives and their staff	10
Put us into high-growth markets (by demographics, geography)	6

Maximize the value of our existing customers and database	6
Minimize the negative impact on existing profit streams	4
Capitalize on market movement to investment products	2
Remove balance sheet constraints	1

At this point, the team took a preliminary vote to prioritize the Driving Forces under consideration; the Low-Cost Production Capability alternative was dropped. Small teams then developed strategic visions based on the remaining three alternatives.

Early on in the evaluation process, team members saw that the Return/Profit alternative was not viable. However, a few were not convinced, and they reserved their right to ask that the alternative be more fully developed and reconsidered later in the process.

The scoring of the two remaining alternatives (both Products Offered, one defined narrowly and one broadly) was completed. There were significant differences. On the question of motivating the CEO and other staff, a narrower definition seemed to cut both ways: While providing a higher comfort level, it was also less exciting for management than a broader focus. Yet the broader focus provided more opportunity to build on the existing base of customers and customer data than its narrower counterpart.

The risk assessment showed that a narrower focus might reduce the company's ability to meet enduring customer needs, creating a loss in revenue. A broader focus indicated that employees would need to acquire new skills and that executives would need to manage product creation and differentiation, something they had been weak at in the past. The broader focus also resembled their current strategy, which had demonstrably failed.

With all the information in hand and after intense debate, the top team formulated a narrow Products Offered framework based on the notion of "Mortgages, savings, and investments. That's all. Nothing else." (Of course, this description was properly fleshed out, but this phrase captures its essence.)

The focus that the Driving Force concept gave to the firm and its successful implementation enabled the company to thrive financially, to be sold at an impressive premium, and to continue to prosper autonomously after it was acquired. This bold move was in sharp contrast to the myriad financial firms that, during the same period, remained diversified beyond recognition and ultimately paid the price.

In another example, Sir Christopher Hogg, when he was chairman of the U.K. conglomerate Courtaulds, provided three strategic "Must" criteria to be considered alongside a range of other objectives for his Fabrics group of companies. Two were financial measures. The third was a constraint on products: For any strategic alternative, the division's products had to remain within the general category of fabrics. The development of nonfabric products, no matter how strategically related or profitable, was not to be considered. This team settled on a course that enabled it to pursue a variety of products—fabrics for apparel, home furnishings, even industrial fabrics—but the parent company's Musts were respected.

THE DRIVING FORCE RULES AND THEIR APPLICATION

Since we defined the original Driving Forces over 20 years ago, we have benefited tremendously from the valuable experiences of our clients. Not surprisingly, our own thinking has also evolved. The original Driving Force concept endures, but a more flexible application has served many organizations well. It is worth noting here the ways in which those central principles have evolved over the years.

Respecting Strategic Autonomy

We encourage the setting of strategy at the divisional, business unit, or even functional levels of an organization. Yet for teams at these levels, choosing a Driving Force can pose a management minefield if done without the umbrella of a corporate strategy.

The best practice, of course, is for a parent to set its strategy and then ensure that its subsidiaries have a certain degree of autonomy to set their own strategy as necessary, although within the parental scope. The mandate to consider strategy for a business unit or division often arises as a project stemming from the parent company's strategy implementation plan. Knowledge about the parent's deliberations and chosen strategic course is essential to the alignment of the dependent unit.

The Driving Force of a subsidiary, division, or business unit must either be compatible with that of its parent, or the parent must have a Return/Profit strategy. A general rule is that subordinate strategies are incompatible if they do not generate synergy with the parent's Driving Force and the conclusions derived from it (namely, product/market scope, the thrust for growth and new business, and the capabilities needed to execute the strategy).

The territory is less murky when the parent's Driving Force is Return/Profit. A Return/Profit holding company (for example, Hanson Trust based equally in the United Kingdom and United States) might provide the umbrella for a Products Offered tobacco company, a brick manufacturer driven by Natural Resources, and an electricity supplier excelling in Method of Distribution. As long as the parent's financial expectations are met, the two strategies need not be compatible.

However, there are very few unfettered Return/Profit organizations. We suspect that even General Electric has certain house rules—for example, its much-publicized objective to be number 1 or number 2 in any sector it chooses to pursue. One company we know had three such guidelines: no international expansion, no high-tech companies, and "no product areas we don't truly understand."

Some organizations that are not Return/Profit driven have such a unity of purpose that all their dependent units will share the same Driving Force: McDonald's, perhaps, or the retailer Benetton. In any location, the product design, look, and feel are the same. One imagines that no regional manager would set strategy differently, for every location offers a "single" product array in a consistent manner to a clearly defined and homogenous market.

Other companies have more difficulty in being strategically cohesive, and some combinations are quite unlikely. In a Products Offered company, a divisional Driving Force of Return/Profit, Technology, or Method of Distribution would be completely at odds with the overall strategy. The division might choose to pursue unrelated products or markets, develop resources and key capabilities that can't be leveraged, or muddy market positioning with contradictory messages. It's a recipe for strategic incoherence and executive conflict.

Similarly, a subsidiary of a Products Offered company cannot have a Markets Served strategy. A company driven by Method of Distribution is very unlikely to have a Technology-driven subsidiary. Quite simply, no organization can afford to go in two directions at the same time. The next chapter examines these ideas in more detail, as we discuss the thrust for growth and new business.

Least fortunate of all are those subsidiaries or divisions whose parent has no strategy. Depending on the organizational structure, they may set strategy without a contextual umbrella—and suffer the potential consequences.

Living with Ambiguity

Another of our original assertions is that there is only one Driving Force for each autonomous organization. Because the Driving Force is defined as the primary determinant of future product and market scope, this is only logical. No matter how close together strategic alternatives score on the decision analysis, the team must make a single choice.

However, the choice of a single Driving Force need not exclude relevant and congruent enhancements based on alternatives that were considered. Strategy teams often gain a fresh perspective when they evaluate other, unchosen Driving Forces. There is no sense in abandoning these lessons learned.

Some organizations tell us they are "80 percent X Driving Force" and "20 percent a combination of Y and Z Driving Forces." This perception is easily understood. For example, we know that any organization seeks a degree of product and brand loyalty from its customers. Every company intends to serve customers as effectively as possible. Yet not every company should base its strategy on the Markets Served Driving Force. Instead, these goals will be met within the framework of the Driving Force that offers the strongest, most robust source of competitive advantage.

At Hallmark International, the team spent several days considering four Driving Force alternatives: Products Offered, Markets Served, Operations Capability, and Method of Distribution. Although Products Offered was the clear and final choice, the team would have been foolish to cast aside the learning and implications derived from considering other alternatives. Through developing four distinct Driving Force scenarios, the team examined its organizational capabilities more closely. Lessons from the Operations Capability alternative revealed the strength of the operational (in this case, creative) capabilities; an effort to boost

Figure 5-1   Lessons from Considering Alternate Driving Forces

the leverage of these resources was built into the strategy. Similarly, in thinking through the Method of Distribution alternative, the team identified areas where adopting new distribution methods would be important.

Incorporating these important sources of insight and support for the strategy did not violate the key thrusts of the organization's Products Offered Driving Force; rather, it resulted in a stronger competitive advantage for the company's future. Today's organizations are not simple. The diagram in Figure 5-1 reflects this reality.

No Standing Still

Former British Prime Minister Harold MacMillan was once asked a parliamentary question by a member of the opposition: Why was the government making a U-turn in its strategy? "Events, dear boy," MacMillan replied. "Events." In response to external or internal events, a company's strategy will evolve over time, necessitating constant review of its Driving Force. The reality is that strategic shifts are rarely scheduled. All organizations evolve over time and may move from one Driving Force to another.

A dramatic evolution occurred at the agricultural equipment company Massey-Ferguson. It was following a Products Offered strategy—the products being agricultural equipment and related components, including diesel engines—when it transformed itself into Varity Corporation through a series of acquisitions, divestments, and consolidations. Varity became an industrial holding company with a wide portfolio of products for the agricultural equipment, automotive, and related industries. It was managed strategically according to what Victor Rice called a "modified" Return/Profit Driving Force—that is, primarily but not exclusively driven by financial criteria. Eventually, Varity sold the agricultural equipment business; it simply did not meet the financial criteria inherent in the new strategy. Varity later merged with Lucas Aerospace to become LucasVarity, a further evolution of its Return/Profit vision. In 1999, LucasVarity was bought by TRW, one of the best examples of a Return/Profit conglomerate.

Another example is Playboy Enterprises, Inc. The Playboy organization had been a one-product company since its founding; its "gentleman's" magazine was known worldwide. Then, as growth slowed and competitive pressure from *Penthouse*, *Hustler*, and similar magazines intensified, it made an apparent shift from Products Offered to Markets Served.

One can imagine that Playboy executives saw the potential in their loyal following as prospects for revenue growth from the magazine declined. Playboy consumers made up a very desirable market niche: They were well-educated, city-dwelling 25- to 55-year-old males with significant disposable income. Many were travelers and businessmen. They were also image conscious, seduced by the Playboy "ethos." They constituted a consumer base whose characteristics showed real synergy—and suggested potential interest in a diverse array of products.

Over a short period of time, Playboy began to offer clubs, casinos, souvenirs, videos, vacation packages, and a variety of other products to these loyal customers. In short, Playboy's synergy had shifted from products to consumers. Its products no longer had anything in common other than their ultimate consumer and the Playboy brand. (Incidentally, whether Playboy actually defined its future in this way is moot. But this scenario, which in our view is entirely plausible, serves as a good example of strategic evolution.)

Knowing Where you Came From

Whether you know it or not, your organization already has a direction. It is already headed somewhere, consciously or not.

When top teams undertake the deliberations described in this chapter, they also identify their present Driving Force and factor it into their considerations. Interestingly, teams are rarely unanimous in identifying the current Driving Force. Some split sharply between alternatives, while others assert that the organization currently follows multiple Driving Forces.

While strategic history can be a useful starting point, teams should not become stuck on this issue. Quite simply, there is frequently insufficient insight to identify correctly the current Driving Force, or the company's strategy (and Driving Force with it) may be in a state of evolution. If this is the case, the team should move on and look to the future.

STRATEGIC WHAT-IF THINKING

For many executive teams, the thinking that is required to select a Driving Force is intense and frustrating, yet rewarding. It is the most intellectually challenging of the strategy process tasks. There is an art to it. It occurs at a conceptual level, and the "right" answers are literally unknowable. The concepts that distinguish Driving Force scenarios are simply that—concepts—and the ultimate test of their efficacy will come only during implementation.

Certain executives on the strategy team will flourish during the work of this phase. Very creative thinkers will welcome the opportunity to develop visionary, even blue-sky scenarios as a way of ensuring that every outside-the-box alternative has been explored. They find the iterative approach—reevaluating, reconsidering at every step—stimulating.

Other executives may find that their strengths lie in the more analytical tasks. They often ensure that strategic objectives are appropriately weighted and alternatives ranked as objectively as possible. In forecasting and analyzing potential risks and opportunities, they contribute enormously to the overall process.

We always find ourselves hoping that there is at least one exceptional writer on the team. The clarity in articulating the conclusions reached is worth its weight in gold. The written articulation (typically a page or two) of the organization's Driving Force is the groundwork for communicating the strategy to others.

Of course, the chief executive is instrumental in the team's success. Often he or she can suggest which individuals might work well together, or how a newcomer's observations or skills might inform the process. Most importantly, he or she role-models the art and discipline required by demonstrating tolerance for creativity and insisting on a disciplined approach to capture the team's collective judgment.

More often than not, thinking about Driving Forces produces significant breakthroughs. We worked with a company that made pharmaceutical products for humans, animals, and agricultural crops—and also made medical devices. Discussing the Products Offered Driving Force prompted one team member to question a formerly taboo area. How on earth, he asked, did medical devices—despite their place in the business mix for over 50 years—fit into this otherwise focused organization? Resources and expertise could not be leveraged from the pharmaceutical areas; in fact, the division required entirely separate sales, manufacturing, and logistical capabilities. Rather than arising from product synergy, the division was simply historical baggage. What's more, the organization's ability to sustain its performance against larger competitors was highly questionable. In a courageous move, the company exited the entire medical devices line.

Years ago, the team at Massey-Ferguson made a similar breakthrough. Its plants manufactured tractors and related equipment within each geographic market—that is, the French made tractors for French farmers, the British for U.K. farmers. The top team realized (under heavy questioning) that all wheat farmers had more in common with each other around the globe than did all farmers within the United Kingdom, or within France. This led to a major reconsideration of product development, the alignment of manufacturing plants, the go-to-market approach, the organization structure, and many other aspects of the strategy.

A Belgian company in the chemical industry needed to determine whether a merger with a competitor made sense. Together, top management from both firms formed a virtual strategy team of six executives from each to develop a strategic profile for the proposed joint company. This exercise in what-if thinking showed to both parties that a merger was not such a good idea; it brought no incremental competitive advantage to either firm. Both therefore remained independent.

This is strategic thinking at its best. It is creative, often painfully so, yet it takes place within the discipline of a shared, rational process. The result is a powerful organizational unity on the foundation for the strategic vision. The fleshing out of that vision is already well underway.

No matter how strong the team, we find that its most effective work is done when we act as independent facilitators. Without facilitation, this task is nearly impossible. Every participant benefits from the requests for further clarification, speculation, or demonstration that only a trusted observer's provocative questions can stimulate.

We will return to the importance of what-if thinking in Chapter 13.

FROM COMPETITIVE ADVANTAGE
TO KEY CAPABILITIES

By its very definition, the Driving Force gets at the heart of a company's strategy, its product and market domain, and—as we'll see in the next chapter—the overall scope and relative emphasis of those products and markets.

The Driving Force decision answers two additional seminal questions: What is the organization's competitive advantage, and which key capabilities will be required to capitalize on it? These components will help make the company's strategic vision a reality as it is translated into action through carefully aligned implementation.

The Driving Forces denote eight unique sources of competitive advantage; each may be interpreted and applied at a corporate level, in a subsidiary, a division, or a function. If the source of competitive advantage shifts over the strategic time frame, the Driving Force is a powerful descriptor of the nature of this evolution. The shift will also require rethinking the organization's key capabilities—that is, the capital resources, skills, information, systems, and processes required to support and exploit the chosen Driving Force.

The electronics firm we mentioned in Chapter 1 was a prime example of this shift in competitive advantage and the implications for its key capabilities. When it was founded, this small international manufacturer of radio-based electronic products was Technology driven. Its competitive advantage lay in its breakthrough radio technology, and its key capabilities were the research and development required to create products based on that technology.

When this firm became our client, several decades after its inception, the team insisted it was still Technology driven. Prominent among the basic beliefs was the statement that the firm would be "first in the realm of technology."

At first tentatively, then more forcefully, these assertions were challenged. Electronics giants like Sony, Motorola, and Philips had consistently overtaken this company's breakthroughs in technology, market share, and products. The firm's products enjoyed only a short shelf life before being superseded, its research cycle was too long, and it had tried to spend its way out of trouble, with draining investments in R&D. Yet it was turning out very few breakthrough products.

The team needed a strategy that would reunify and invigorate the company. After a painful series of discussions, it finally agreed to settle for a key basic belief: "It is better to be *best* than *first*." The Technology Driving Force was then ruled out because in the Driving Force discussion, it implied being "first," which was no longer a tenable position.

The implications for shifting the company's resources were clear. In a Technology-driven company, for example, hiring the best and the brightest innovators is a key capability. For this electronics firm, that intent was no longer realistic.

The team settled on a Products Offered Driving Force. That choice, along with other strategic parameters, committed the team to pursuing "best-in-class" products, and overall product quality was identified as the primary competitive advantage.

When Keith Alm's team settled on a Products Offered Driving Force, it identified two components of its competitive advantage: understanding current and prospective consumer needs better than any competitor, and meeting those needs through the efforts of the world's best creative resources.

Hallmark International's key capabilities then were self-evident: outstanding market research to understand its consumers' needs and attracting best-of-the-best creative and editorial staff. Although it could also draw on best-practice manufacturing resources, this capability was less important. In fact, the outsourcing of production has become increasingly common throughout Hallmark.

The Driving Force helps companies identify a locus for its competitive advantage—that is, for a Products Offered company, the competitive advantage will pertain to characteristics of the products themselves. Teams then ask, "What is unique about our company vis-à-vis our products? What are our sources of uniqueness and product differentiation?" These questions provide clues that help to further clarify the competitive advantage. Similarly, a Technology-driven company is sure to find its locus of competitive advantage in its technologies and their applications.

Like the team at Hallmark, most organizations find that they have no more than two or three key capabilities that are absolutely essential to the success of their strategy, and it is to these that their resources are directed. Other capabilities are of secondary importance and in many companies are outsourced.

LOOKING BACK

Clearly, no organization can duck these central questions about its nature and direction:

- What, exactly, is our organization about? What is its unifying force? What drives our forward impetus? How do we describe the central focus of our business activities? What will ensure that the efforts of our organization as a whole are aligned with our purpose?
- What is the primary basis for determining the scope of our products and markets?
- What is our major source of competitive advantage?
- Which must-have capabilities are key to our strategic success?
- What will guide our crucial decisions on which areas should be pursued to provide growth and opportunities for new business?
- How will we make the tough decisions on allocating and deploying our valuable yet inevitably limited resources? On what basis will we make day-to-day decisions, balancing operational imperatives with our strategic focus and sense of purpose?
- In what ways should our corporate culture reflect the strategic imperatives we follow? How will we describe, monitor, and reward human performance in light of those imperatives? What are the fundamental messages that should be communicated internally and externally to make strategy implementation possible?
- How will our various subsidiaries and/or functional areas chart their own course for the future?
- What is the strategic intent of our competitors? Which Driving Force might they have adopted, and what does this say about

their basis for competitive advantage? What proactive counter-measures might we take in light of this understanding?

- What framework will support the evolution of our strategy over the strategic time frame? How will we continually renew our strategy, reexamining and confirming the alternatives we have chosen?

The Driving Force concept addresses these questions and establishes the foundation for action.

We challenge you to consider the eight Driving Forces as they relate to your own organization. Consider the primary drivers of decision making in your company now: What might they indicate about your current Driving Force? When you envision your company's evolution over the next several years, what shifts are likely to be most compelling and rewarding? What are the implications for your selection of a Driving Force for the future? Which Driving Force describes the locus for competitive advantage that you anticipate will carry the organization forward?

The steps leading to the selection of a Driving Force have called for the toughest thinking a strategy team will do—that of creating alternative futures. The next tasks are to spell out the relative emphasis of product and market combinations, determine their financial mix, and set priorities for growth and new business. This is followed by an assessment of the growth and return expectations required by the top team, to include revenue, profit, return on investment, cash generation, and also market-related metrics such as volume and share.

6

Strategy Formulation: Completing the Roadmap

Just recently, we were with the senior management team of a well-known service organization in the European health care industry. Some of these executives were arguing against the need for revisiting the organization's strategy. The company's direction, they felt, was very clear to all concerned.

We sketched out the matrix in Figure 6-1, which serves to map the company's broad intentions for growth and new business. The nine cells show the intersection of products and markets in three general categories. We then asked each individual to number the nine cells to indicate their relative priority in the company's thrust for growth and new business. Would it move first to offer current products to extended or new markets? Or would it create entirely new products to take to its existing markets? Would it be brave and go for new products to new markets?

Every one of the six replies was different. The answers revealed that, not only did the team lack cohesion on the company's strategic priorities, but it also had no shared view of the current Driving Force. Products Offered? Markets Served? A Return/Profit holding company? Anything and everything was plausible, according to their sketches.

In the previous chapter, we explored the power of the Driving Force concept in helping an organization establish unity and purpose, articulate its competitive advantage, and identify key capabilities. Now we

Products/Services

	Current	Modified	Entirely New
Markets — Current			
Markets — Extended			
Markets — Entirely New			

	Products/Services	**Markets**
Current	Products with shared characteristics, meeting the same enduring need, now being sold/delivered	Markets (geographies, customers, end users) with shared characteristics, now being served
Modified/ Extended	Engineered/developed/improved products with similar characteristics	Different markets with essentially similar characteristics
Entirely New *(for this company)*	Products with significantly different characteristics meeting entirely different needs	Markets with significantly different characteristics, e.g., demographics, geographies, buying patterns

Figure 6-1   The Nine-Box Matrix: Thrust for Growth and New Business

turn to the remaining considerations for completing a strategic profile. For each of these components, the Driving Force serves as the starting point for determining a common direction. The statement of Driving Force largely determines the organization's product and market momentum, and thus it has significant implications for the thrust for growth and new business, optimum segmentation of products and markets, and their relative emphasis. The Driving Force also plays a key part in the decisions made about financial expectations.

In turn, these components enrich and inform the considerations that have gone before. For example, we have seen teams establish their strategic time frame—say, 3 or 4 years—but when they delineate specific product and market efforts, they see that either the time frame must be extended or their strategic ambitions curbed. Similarly, the statement of Driving Force is often clarified as the team completes its product and market deliberations.

Again, the task of formulating strategy is rarely linear; most teams spend considerable effort in reviewing and revisiting each component until they are satisfied.

Many of the examples in this chapter are based on companies that remain unnamed. These more explicit areas of strategy—specific priorities for new growth, product/market segmentation, and financial benchmarks—are closely guarded in most organizations, and we respect their privacy. Nonetheless, the examples accurately represent our experiences.

FROM DRIVING FORCE TO PRODUCTS AND MARKETS

To move from the statement of Driving Force to an actionable plan, every strategy team must envision its future business on several different levels. First, it must establish the organization's thrust and priorities for growth and new business. Second, it must outline the specific product categories to be offered and markets to be served. This includes determining their part in the relative emphasis and financial mix of the business and how each will contribute to the success of the strategy.

Describing the Thrust for Growth and New Business

The nine-box matrix works in three ways. First, it describes the boundaries between the nature of products and markets that will be strategically "in" and "out" to limit the future playing field. Second, it is directional; the priority ranking of each cell portrays the overall thrust for growth and new business and relative priority of certain areas. Finally, the matrix helps to clarify which areas will be pursued first and which later over the strategic time period.

Lessons from the Driving Force

One of the toughest questions a top team faces is how it will move out of its comfort zone of current products and markets. The team must turn for guidance to its choice of Driving Force, for each of the eight we discussed in the previous chapter has specific implications for an organization's thrust for growth and new business.

Though any company might welcome opportunities to pursue both new products and new markets immediately, only one that has no conflicting demands on capital investment and other resources and which has no specific direction suggested by its Driving Force can do so. Very few of these exist, and they are always Return/Profit driven. Just as the choice of a Driving Force helps the team to focus its strategic attention, this matrix helps it take the next step in defining that focus.

There are certain Rubicons that are suggested by the matrix, the boundaries of which are indicated by an organization's Driving Force. It is unlikely that any organization will cross more than one of these, unless it is Return/Profit driven. These Rubicons are illustrated in Figure 6-2. Interestingly, too many organizations ignore the opportunity to fully exploit and penetrate the current products/current markets cell first, preferring the risk of placing first priority in fields where new business opportunities seem more attractive.

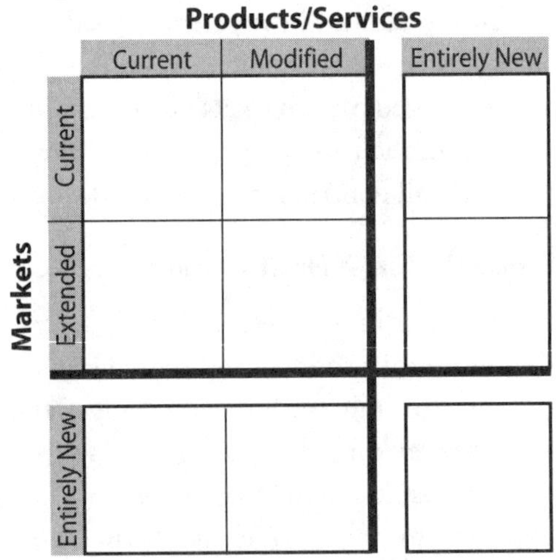

Figure 6-2 Thrust for Growth and New Business: The Rubicons

Thus a Products Offered organization, for example, draws its strength from the synergy generated among its current and future products, which are offered to meet a common, enduring customer need. A typical Products Offered organization may have these priorities:

1. Exploit current products and current markets.
2. Offer current products to extended markets.

3. Offer modified products to current markets.
4. Offer modified products to extended markets.
5. Offer current products to new markets.

A Products Offered company is unlikely to cross the Rubicon into entirely new products that meet a different need.

Imagine yourself a fly on the wall at a Products Offered automobile manufacturer. When its top management team talks of the existing family car or sedan model, its year-to-year upgrade, and perhaps even a station wagon version, they are addressing the "current" product line. The products may be slightly different, but they meet the same fundamental need. A foray into sports utility vehicles or lightweight pickup trucks might represent the pursuit of "modified" products. But if the talk turns to manufacturing motorcycles, or tractors, or even a wide variety of automobile components—seat fabrics, tires, and CD players, for example—the "new-product Rubicon" will have been crossed. Such pursuits will indicate that the company's Driving Force has changed or should be significantly reframed.

The story is different for a Markets Served firm. To return to our example from the last chapter, the Playboy organization would be very unlikely to offer its current products to an entirely new consumer market, as it would have little in common with the current market. Therefore, don't expect to see Playboy taking its products to new socio-economic groups, and certainly not to new demographic groups (to children, for example—demographically new, but unethical and implausible). More likely would be an offering targeted to a similar but new consumer group in existing geographic markets; for example, the company has targeted women with the same socioeconomic characteristics as their male counterparts by offering them *Playboy*-type magazines.

The new-product and new-market Rubicons of the growth and new-business matrix do not just apply to companies with a Driving Force of Markets Served or Products Offered, however.

Think of the U.S. Forest Service, quite probably a Natural Resource–driven organization. It has a broad range of current products and services, from wood to wood-pulp and paper products. Yet, because its Driving Force relates directly to the source of its products, it is not likely to cross the new-products Rubicon. The Forest Service is not likely to venture into product areas based on electronic media, for example.

However, it might exploit its resources more fully and venture into products and services new to the organization. Thus, it may offer recreational services, meeting an entirely different need, yet founded on its command of large tracts of land.

The capabilities-based Driving Forces show similar parallels. In the early 1970s Xerox Corporation showed characteristics of a Technology Driving Force. For 2 decades, Xerox did not cross the new-products Rubicon since its competitive advantage lay in a body of knowledge and research around xerographic products. When its patents began to expire, competitive pressures forced Xerox into nonxerographic products (e.g., fax machines, office supplies)—a move that in our view changed its Driving Force to Products Offered, with its domain located in a wide variety of office products.

Avon, which may have a Method of Sale Driving Force, would be unlikely to cross a new-markets Rubicon. Marketing to a customer group with entirely new characteristics—high-net-worth individuals, for example—would require a shift away from the closely networked, in-home approach that defines its strength. Avon is much more likely to develop new business through offering new products to meet the changing needs of its core customer base.

The Return/Profit organization is the exception here. If its only constraints are financial ones, there is no prohibition against entering a new product area and/or new markets. Return/Profit organizations pursue new business in any area they please, provided that they meet their financial hurdle rates. The Rubicons do not apply.

Basic Principles of Growth and New Business

The organization's Driving Force implies that only one or the other of the Rubicons—new products or new markets—is likely to be crossed. With the exception of Return/Profit–driven firms, organizations will generally address priorities that include only four to six of the nine cells during the strategic time frame. The matrix in Figure 6-3 shows these principles.

Realism and Gray Areas

The principles are not intended to be totally inflexible. The matrix cannot necessarily reflect the complexity of a given organization. Most

Each strategic Rubicon separates current and modified products from entirely new products, and current and extended markets from entirely new markets. Determining the organization's exact thrust for growth and new business lies in the priority assigned to each of the four to six boxes the company will pursue.

Products/Services

	Current	Modified	Entirely New
Current	A	B	C
Extended	B	B	C
Entirely New	C	C	D

Markets

A Every organization has current markets and products. Companies should seek to maximize opportunities in this area before venturing further.

B Most organizations will pursue current and modified products, and/or current and extended markets, early in the strategic period.

C Many organizations will eventually aspire to address *either* products/ services entirely new to them, or entirely new markets.

D Few organizations will be able to take new products to new markets.

Figure 6-3 Thrust for Growth and New Business: Priorities

companies will encounter gray areas that challenge the principle that the "Rubicon should not be crossed."

When an organization sees a relatively risk-free and potentially profitable opportunity to explore an area where the construct suggests it should "never" go, how firm should it stand?

If it pursues such an opportunity, the top team must clearly demarcate this area as outside the core business, continually test its implications for the core strategy (particularly the siphoning off of key resources), monitor results closely, and be brave enough to pull the plug on the venture if need be. Some firms might also explore such an opportunity to test the viability of a strategic shift without undertaking a wholesale reorientation.

We saw this approach in practice, when Massey-Ferguson became Varity Corporation and considered several moves into new product areas. Although it didn't go into either brothels or ice cream (!), it did set up a separate division devoted to new ventures. Its purpose was to explore products in noncore areas to see whether they might be successful and/or generate synergies with core products. This division was ring fenced, reported its own profit-and-loss statement, and ensured that these ventures were closely monitored.

There are no absolutes; each company is different. But if this crossing of the Rubicon becomes a habit, the Driving Force or the discipline of its implementation must be reevaluated.

The diagrams in Figure 6-4 are realistic depictions of the thrust for growth and new business of Products Offered and Markets Served organizations.

The Role of Return/Growth Expectations

At this juncture, the strategy team must consider the financial goals that it expects to achieve as the result of its new strategy. As we've noted, every organization has a raison d'être that stands apart from its financial goals (except of course our purely Return/Profit-driven friends).

Yet the financial fundamentals—revenue growth, providing return to shareholders, reinvesting in the business, reducing a debt burden, sharing profits with employees—are an integral part of every vision. In strategic terms, they are an output of, rather than the prime motive behind, the strategy.

Developing these goals is, like the overall process, iterative. Financial indicators are first discussed during the gathering of strategic intelligence, when expectations from the parent company and/or shareholders are examined. If need be, this line of inquiry may be pursued; the team may scrutinize more closely its industry's financial benchmarks, its shareholders' expectations, or the macroeconomic trends identified in Phase 1.

A statement of financial expectations will also be iterative with the next task, that of segmenting products and markets and determining their relative emphasis and financial mix. One company used a version of the growth and new-business matrix to help make these connections. It expressed shifts in business priorities as a percentage of revenue, as shown in Figure 6-5. The top team immediately saw that the company would be relying on entirely new markets for 13 percent of its revenue—with a corresponding decrease in emphasis on existing products. For this company, it was the first step in translating a high level of

PRODUCTS OFFERED DRIVING FORCE

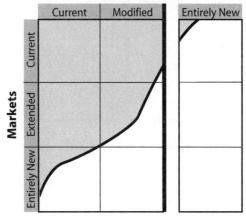

**The Rubicon is unlikely
to be crossed
(entirely new products,
or entirely new markets)**

MARKETS SERVED DRIVING FORCE

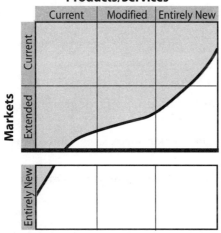

Figure 6-4 Thrust for Growth and New Business: Driving Forces

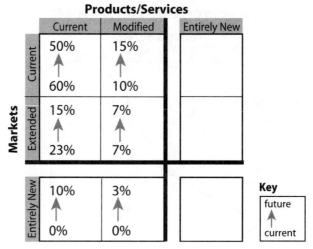

Figure 6-5 Shifts in Business Priorities

strategic intent into a detailed product/market matrix to test its thinking around revenue targets.

Financial expectations include the following types of parameters:

- Return on investment (or capital, or assets managed) or a similar metric
- Profit targets [earnings before interest and taxes (EBIT), earnings before interest, taxes, depreciation, and amortization (EBITDA), or net after taxes, for example]
- Cash flow requirements

Also included are general parameters for growth, expressed as:

- Increased revenue, market share, sales volume, customers served, and so on
- Improved performance from one year to the next on each of the parameters

Many senior executives breathe a sigh of relief at this stage in the process, because they're most comfortable working with the financial constructs of their company. Yet these are not financial plans or projections but financial goals that describe an ideal future. Ultimately, the team must judge what the company's financial results *should* be.

The comfort zone is short lived, but this level of thinking forces the team to work iteratively with the Driving Force, basic beliefs, time frame, and growth and new-business concepts to establish some financial parameters. Other factors also affect the relative importance of financial expectations. For example, if a company plans to develop either new revenue or new capabilities through acquisition, it must ensure that its goals provide for the accumulation of capital, the ability to raise cash, or share swapping.

At the Savoy Group of Hotels, one important financial insight was the existing "suboptimization" of assets—in its case, the hotel rooms and facilities. Each of its products and services—rooms, food, telephone connections, laundry, and so on—had a very different range of profitability. For this team, the challenge lay in juggling the product mix to raise profits overall. This called for changing the emphasis on various product lines. In relative terms, for example, rooms constituted the largest share of the revenue mix, but a significantly smaller proportion of the profit mix. Alcoholic beverages, on the other hand, provided better profit margins. The solution was not to focus on beverages but to take a hard look at improving the leverage on its most important and expensive assets, the hotel buildings.

This work of establishing financial goals should not be confused with detailed business planning. Rather, the results of these deliberations define a roadmap to future sources of revenue and profit. They drive business plans, and they are one of the key indicators for monitoring the success of the strategy. They also are used to validate the financial mix of the proposed product/market combinations to which we now turn.

CREATING THE PRODUCT/MARKET MATRIX

If the organization's strategic vision represents its corporate nirvana, then the product/market matrix is its roadmap for getting there. It provides a means for managing strategy implementation through determining the relative emphasis to be placed on each product/market grouping. It allows an enterprise to allocate its scarce resources to implementation efforts in a way that is consistent with exploiting its competitive advantage.

As noted, the matrix is also an input to return and growth expectations, as well as a reality test of them. Thus, expectations are crafted concurrently and iteratively with the matrix.

There are four distinct tasks:

- Define and segment current and possible future products and markets that will be pursued over the course of the strategic period.
- Determine the criteria for assigning relative emphasis to specific product/market combinations.
- Assess each cell to establish the appropriate degree of future emphasis, its current emphasis, the type of emphasis, the difficulty anticipated in making the shift, and financial expectations.
- Review the matrix and overall strategy to test them against strategic intelligence and the team's best judgment of its reality.

Segmenting Products and Markets

The first step in creating the product/market matrix is to divide or segment products and markets into strategically or operationally significant, common groupings. Much has been written about the specifics of segmentation, and we will not analyze the advantages of various methods here. However, the major segmentation variables for both the product and market axes are determined by the organization's Driving Force; it describes the nature and characteristics of the products and markets within the organization's scope. Categorization by these variables ensures that segments will share a natural synergy. Further clues are provided by the organization's competitive advantage.

The goal is to identify related, manageable entities for implementing the strategy. These are the organizing principles for your product/market reality.

In addition to the guidance provided by the Driving Force, questions that help teams characterize product segments include:

- What is this product's (or product category's) end use or application?
- What are the marketing and performance characteristics of the product (for example, pricing, packaging, quality, service)?

- What are its unique features and benefits? How is it differentiated from other products in the marketplace, and to what degree?

Questions that help identify distinct market segments include:

- Is our initial segmentation based on geography, customers, or end users?
- What shared characteristics does this market segment have? What demographic features do its constituents share?
- What are the buying motives, purchasing patterns, and performance requirements for this market segment?
- What are the channels for distribution to this market? Do we have a retail, wholesale, Internet, or direct relationship with this market?

International firms may have to make an initial geographic cut of markets before they can further segment them. Whenever the characteristics of a company's markets vary significantly from country to country, a geographic first-cut is often required. Then separate matrices are created for each country; the market axis is country specific while the products are the same for each country.

The challenge in segmentation is keeping it strategic, rather than letting the process become a tactical planning exercise more appropriate for product or market managers. Just imagine the team at Procter & Gamble, with its thousands of products, 160 geographic markets, and diverse customer segments within each of those markets. At P&G, product segmentation at a strategic level would help the team home in on the relative importance of broad product categories, such as detergent and dish soap, or of the Western European, U.S., and Southeast Asian markets.

A sound matrix gives directional clues that guide operations management, without dictating the details. In our experience, most teams end up with a matrix that has between 100 and 200 cells.

The final segmentation should include both existing products and customers and all possible future products and customers consistent with the strategy. Not all of these will be addressed over the strategic time frame, and some will not be applicable (for example, lipstick for men). The boundaries of the matrix should match the product/market scope. Products or customers inappropriate for the future strategy fall outside the matrix.

In a rare case, one strategy team insisted on having a matrix of about 300 active cells. It had just 8 customer (market) categories, but 35 or so major product categories. It insisted on working as a full group to apply more than a dozen criteria to the assessment of every cell. Surely, this had crossed over the line between a strategic vision and a tactical exercise. After spinning its wheels for 2 full days, this team gave up. Its thinking was not sophisticated enough to ensure the strategy's success.

When the segmentation structure accurately reflects an organization's strategic intent, as opposed to its more common use as a tactical marketing and sales technique, then each cell represents an important strategic message and call to arms.

Criteria for Assessing Product/Market Cells

Based on the work thus far—the results of the strategic intelligence gathering and analysis, the selection of the Driving Force, the organization's competitive advantage and key capabilities, the basic beliefs, and initial financial targets—the strategy team establishes the criteria for assessing the relative role of each cell in the resulting product/market mix.

The process is analogous to that of selecting a Driving Force. Questions that help set criteria include:

- What are our existing product/market activities? How successful have they been, and what do we expect in the future?
- What have our Driving Force discussions revealed about our organization's overall direction?
- What is our general thrust for growing the business?
- Which capabilities are currently strengths? Which must we build or acquire?

Assessment criteria vary widely between organizations. Here is a partial list one company used to assess the relative importance of its many geographic markets:

Criterion	Relative Weight (1–10, 10 = Highest)
Highest number of economically viable consumers	10
Greatest revenue potential	8
Greatest consumer brand leverage ability	7
Best external supply chain infrastructures	5
Opportunities to be the market leader	4
Fewest external economic and political risks	3

Ask yourself this question: Which criteria would I expect my top team to use in determining relative priorities for product and market combinations? How are these decisions currently made?

The following example, depicted in Figure 6-6, illustrates a systematically created product/market matrix that is aligned with a specific Driving Force. As you study the matrix, look for areas that parallel your own company. What would your own product/market matrix look like? How would you describe the shift, if any, intended in future emphasis for certain product/market cells? And what are the implications for the capabilities your organization currently has or will need to develop?

Example: An Initial Product/Market Matrix

This matrix represents a portion of one developed some years ago by a major beverage distribution company in a small European country. The company had chosen a Method of Distribution Driving Force; it determined that its overall thrust for growth and new business was based on increasing the number of products made available to key customer groups. It sought to exploit the competitive advantage inherent in its trucking, logistics, and overall distribution system. The company's trucks made frequent deliveries to every establishment in the country. Thus, it chose to grow through offering modified products (coffee, tea, and milk), and products entirely new to them, such as snack foods, to existing markets with which it had had a long-standing exemplary relationship. These modified and new products were outsourced since the firm had no capability or desire to produce them in-house.

Current Markets			Alcohol			Sodas		Juices		Modified Products	Entirely New Products	Total Overall Customer Emphasis
			Beer	Wine	Spirits	Coke Clones	Others	Organic	Standard	Coffee, Tea, Milk	Non-beverage: Nuts, Chips, Pretzels, Cookies	
Retailers	Supermarkets		H **D** / M	H **D** / M	L **PD** / M	M **S** / M	L **S** / L	H **D** / L	L / M	**E** / O	L **D** / O	H / M
	Specialty		H **S** / H	M **D** / L	M **S** / M	L **S** / L	L **S** / L	M **D** / O	L / L	**E** / O	L **D** / O	M / M
	Corner Shops		N/A	N/A	N/A	L **PD** / M	L **S** / L	L **D** / O	L / L	**E** / O	L **D** / O	M / M
Pubs	Chains		H **D** / H	H **D** / M	M **PD** / H	M **S** / M	L **S** / L	L **D** / O	L **PD** / M	**D** M / O	L **D** / O	H / M
	Independents		H **D** / H	H **D** / M	M **PD** / H	M **S** / M	L **S** / L	L **D** / O	L **PD** / M	**D** M / O	L **D** / O	M / M
Government	Educational Establishments		N/A	N/A	N/A	L **PD** / M	L **PD** / M	L / H	L **PD** / M	**E** L / O	**E** O / O	L / M
	Hospitals		L **S** / L	M **D** / L	O **PD** / L	L **S** / L	L **S** / L	H **D** / L	L **PD** / M	**D** H / M	**E** O / O	M / L
	Retirement Homes		L **S** / L	M **D** / L	L **S** / L	L **S** / L	L **S** / L	H **D** / L	L **PD** / M	**D** M / H	M / O	M / L
Total Overall Product Emphasis			H / H	H / M	M / H	L / M	L / L	H / L	L / M	M / O	L / O	

Key

Degree of Emphasis
H = High
M = Medium
L = Low
N/A = Not applicable, e.g. lipstick to men
0 = Choose not to pursue at this time

future **X** ← current

Type of Emphasis
D = Develop
S = Sustain current effort
OPP = Opportunistic
M = Monitor
E = Explore
PD = Phase Down

Figure 6-6 Example of a Product/Market Matrix

This matrix typifies a number of important features:

- Modified and new products were added based on the company's chosen Driving Force. In considering the competitive advantage (i.e., what other products could be tied into our distribution capability), the product range was expanded (i.e., which other beverages might we offer, which other products are naturally paired with beverages).
- The matrix shows two levels of segmentation. (In this example, only two of three levels are shown; for example, educational institutions are one market segment within the government category; further segmentation defined kindergartens, schools, and colleges as specific markets.)
- The matrix provides an overview of future emphasis (High, Medium, and Low) not only by cell but also by general product and customer groups (see columns for total customer and total product emphasis). Sometimes firms complete these product columns and market rows first so as to put a stake in the ground before addressing each cell.
- The matrix helps identify how a shift in emphasis for a product or market segment affects the emphasis on other segments. (In this example, a shift toward organic juices implies a deemphasis for both standard juices and sodas. The importance of the retirement home segment is also consistent across a range of products.)
- Working through the matrix revealed new markets that could realistically be added to the company's domain. In this case, the next logical thrust to be considered was the adoption of an international scope.

Each cell describes the planned position at the end of the time frame. The future *degree of emphasis* (top management time, attention, and effort, as well as the resources required for execution) is considered first, so that the team's visioning is not based on current activities. The *type of emphasis* describes the nature of the action needed to attain the intended targets.

A Detailed Roadmap

Using the criteria established for assessing product/market emphasis, the strategy team now formulates its specific expectations. In effect, it conducts a small-scale decision analysis on the future activity for each

For each product/market cell, detailed variables such as the
metrics for success, target date, and degree of difficulty
may be added to the information on current, future,
and type of emphasis.

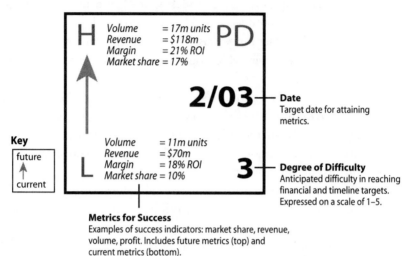

Figure 6-7 Example of Completed Product/Market Cell

cell. This reflects the contribution each product/market combination
makes to the organization's strategic intent. Most teams find that the
task requires a combination of disciplined assessment against the criteria, an intuitive view of the relative role of certain cells, and a final review
to assure reasonable balance among the cells.

The result will include indicators for each product/market cell, as
shown in Figure 6-7.

Auditing the Product/Market Roadmap

Teams encounter a number of pitfalls in creating a product/market
matrix.

First, they invariably find that, after a first pass at assigning the degree
of future emphasis, there are too many Hs—segments that require a
High (H) degree of emphasis and therefore an allocation of inevitably
scarce resources.

In tandem with this, we often see that far too many segments call
for a Developmental emphasis, which will also strain the company's
resources. Some first drafts of the product/market matrix may call for
30 to 50 percent of their cells to receive this kind of attention.

Either of these common problems has the same result—a matrix whose balance between cells in each category of emphasis and degree of difficulty is not appropriate or realistic. The team's work will be for naught if the outcome is an unobtainable wish list rather than a route to reality.

To ensure the validity of the matrix, we suggest that companies look for these strategic "red flags":

- Do we have an overall balance between cells that will receive High (H), Medium (M), and Low (L) emphasis? Is there a reasonable bell-shaped curve in their distribution?
- Is the number of shifts in emphasis manageable?
- Is the matrix populated with a large number of Opportunistic and Explore cells? Do we understand the risk that the energy and resources used to investigate cells may lead nowhere in the long run?

There is always a certain amount of give and take inherent in this audit process, but the team must keep a disciplined, strategic focus.

When individual cells or groups of cells seem to threaten the balance, they should be flagged for further consideration. The team should focus on the cells that are pivotal and test (as far as possible) its assumptions in those areas. Such testing should encompass only what is feasible, both practically and financially. Ultimately, however, the validity of the matrix will be known only when the strategy begins to be implemented.

The simplest test is one of observation and reflection: Simply, can the expectations expressed in this cell and the matrix as a whole be met? Again, we are in the realm of the future, and the future is unknowable; it is best assessed through research and analysis when possible, judgment, and disciplined, rigorous process thinking. Strategy will be an unfolding reality in any company because it involves elements outside the company's control. Of course, any number of wildly successful—and unsuccessful—products have contradicted the finest market research. The Sony Walkman, for example, was never tested on potential markets. Its creation—and enthusiastic reception by millions of end users—was quite simply the result of sheer inspiration. And the rejection of the "new Coke" phenomenon a decade ago proved that market researchers are not always right.

The strategy team at Bristol and West Bank audited its product/market matrix in a creative and disciplined fashion. It completed the segmentation and assessment of each cell for the last year of its strategic time frame, and then created another matrix to represent each of the preceding years, returning to its present state. It demonstrated its ability to work strategically, with the future as its starting point. This approach proved extremely powerful for management decision making throughout the strategic time frame, and was used as a "given" by the planning community.

What is the relationship between the overall expectations for return and profit and the financial targets assigned to each product/market cell? The matrix is a reality check, intended to demonstrate that overall financial objectives can be met. To review this alignment, most top teams paint the product/market targets in fairly broad strokes, then turn to internal marketing and financial leaders to work through the math as an interim task. When the team does its final review, it must ensure that successful implementation of its product/market intentions will deliver the required financial results.

Finally, the product/market matrix should be compared with the team's articulation of the Driving Force. This will ensure that the intuition of the team has been tempered with its disciplined statement of focus for the future.

Progress in implementing the matrix will be a key indicator of strategic success. Similarly, each cell that entails a shift in emphasis represents a project in itself, such projects being part of the overall Strategic Master Project Plan to be discussed in Chapter 8.

Strategic Implications of the Product/Market Matrix

When completed, the product/market matrix is the heart of the strategic profile and the explicit roadmap for its implementation. Thus the matrix should be audited to ensure that the team has wrestled with the following tough questions:

- Which of our current product groups and markets will increase in relative emphasis?
- Which will we deemphasize, though they may have served us well in the past?
- What current activities will be sustained in the future?

- What will be the relative effort focused on exploring entirely new product/market combinations?
- What is the relative future importance of the revenue mix we expect from these entirely new cells?

The matrix is also the key to understanding and codifying the specific actions that will move the strategy forward. As the team turns to the challenge of implementation, answers to the following questions may be inferred from the information contained in the product/market matrix:

- Which capabilities will be most critical to pursuing the shift from our current activities to those in our vision of the future? (One critical capability that is often overlooked is the ability to execute Phase Down efforts.)
- Which capabilities will we need to develop, acquire, or outsource?
- What skills and behaviors will our people need to bring about this vision of the future?
- What are the implications for the structure of our organization?
- Where might we realize improved clarity, synergy, and economies of scale?
- How will we communicate our vision internally and help each employee grasp and act on the strategic requirements for change?
- What messages will we need to share with our stakeholders, our suppliers, our customers, and the media about our strategic intentions?

CHARACTERISTICS OF A STRATEGIC PROFILE

Throughout the formulation process, teams will have articulated, recorded, and refined every facet of the strategic vision. So much material has usually accumulated by this time that most teams need to pause to see how the profile is taking shape.

The best strategic profiles, in our experience, share a number of characteristics. Every strategy team should review its work to ensure that the profile meets these expectations.

- Have we used a rigorous, visible, and shared process to create our strategic vision?
- Do we have common ownership of the vision?
- Do we share a commitment to its implementation?
- Is our statement clear and concise (typically no more than 10 to 12 pages)? Is it easily understood? Can each of us "carry it in our heads"?
- Can we communicate this vision effectively to the rest of the organization? Will it motivate and unite us? For our key employees, does it answer the questions "What is my role in executing our strategy" and "What does this mean for me?"
- Do we understand how to apply our vision in the organization? Can it be used to guide day-to-day decision making?
- Does it explain which products and markets will be considered high priority in allocating our scarce yet valuable resources?
- Is our vision realistic? Can we implement it? Have we avoided making blue-sky or ambiguous statements?
- Is this vision compatible with our corporate culture? Do we understand what changes may be needed for successful implementation?
- Can our strategic success be monitored and measured? Do we understand how we will monitor shifts in external and internal assumptions, as well as our performance in implementation? Do we know how we will update it based on this?

When the team can answer these questions with a resounding yes, it is ready to dig in to the nitty-gritty of making its vision a reality through excellence in implementation.

The tracking mechanisms needed to provide performance metrics will already have been discussed throughout the strategy process, and they are unique to the nature of each organization. We call these metrics *Key Indicators of Strategic Success.* The requirement for discipline in this area is a given; perhaps less obvious are these precautions:

- Avoid creating a system in which significant facts and trends are lost in the complexity and detail of the reports.
- Beware the temptation to focus solely on financial results; other indicators are equally meaningful.

- Ensure that the metrics reflect performance on strategic priorities rather than on operational effectiveness.
- Keep the system straightforward and user friendly. If the statistics require extraordinary effort to produce, either by managers or an already-burdened IT department, accuracy will eventually be sacrificed and the measures no longer taken seriously.
- Finally, remember that information alone is of no particular use; implications must be drawn from it and incorporated into the strategic thinking of the top team.

We will return to the question of how to review, monitor, and update strategic success in Chapter 12.

UNIQUE CEO ROLE IN STRATEGY FORMULATION

By the time a team has begun formulating strategy, the CEO will have already made two key decisions: choosing the members of the strategy team, and choosing a sound process for completing the five phases of strategy.

Although a CEO's insights and expertise in content-related areas will be valuable, his or her responsibility to the team and the process as a whole will significantly impact the outcome. Inevitably, the CEO must carefully address the following questions:

Which members of the team have emerged as its real thought leaders? Are they in roles that utilize the best of their strategic thinking? What is the overall quality of their strategic thinking? Are we missing any contributors who would improve the outcome? Keith Alm at Hallmark International let the makeup of his strategy team evolve over time, as he monitored the capabilities of his people and their contribution to the team's thinking. When the idea of cell phone greetings was conceived, he immediately added the individual who had been identified as the person to undertake exploratory work in that area.

One team struggled with a participant who was a content expert but found it tough to work in a group environment. He was brilliant but a rather opinionated loner. Eventually, he was asked to leave, although he and his colleagues were consulted on content as needed. This move gave the remaining team the breathing room it needed to move forward.

What are the forces at work beyond the scope of my top team? Have I had "grandfather chats" at the next level in the hierarchy, for example with the board chairman, to illuminate larger issues that impact our work, or have I asked our facilitators to do so? The Royal Mail reformulated its strategy at an extraordinary time. It was during and after the 1992 general election, and there was considerable debate as to whether the Conservative government, if reelected, would privatize the Post Office, the Royal Mail's parent. Though our project was with the chief executive and his team, I agreed to meet every month with the chairman (who reported to the secretary of state), one on one. Given the chief executive's position in the spotlight, and the landmines behind the scenes, it was important to have another channel for testing the strategy's validity in light of these outside political pressures.

As CEO, have I done everything possible to support breakthrough thinking and creativity? Have we reached a level of strategic thinking that is beyond the ordinary and the rational? Have I ensured that we are visionaries, not planners? As many have noted, the greatest strategies are those that are not anticipated by the competition. The element of surprise may not be reached through rational analysis alone. The fostering of an open, breakthrough environment increases the chance that this will happen. The CEO also helps ensure that the team's work does not devolve into the realms of projections, financial analysis, and long-range planning. A strong leader will help his or her team stay focused on vision.

If the team is struggling, do I have the courage to exercise my own leadership prerogative? Do I recognize that, as primus inter pares *(first among equals), the buck stops here?* The chief executive of a pharmaceutical company which is now owned by Rhone Poulenc eventually reached the limit of his endurance. Over several days, his team had worked through alternative strategic visions based on three or four Driving Forces. After much heated but well-informed debate, it had narrowed the choice to two. And the team members were absolutely deadlocked.

At the end of one afternoon, this distraught executive literally backed me up against a wall. "What am I supposed to do?" he roared.

After a bit of calming, he headed home for a sleepless night, finally understanding that it was time for him to make the final decision. The next morning we helped him test his rationale and craft a few words to help him present his decision to the team, yet we offered no definitive answer on the correct Driving Force. This team needed to see that its leader was willing and able to make the tough call himself. It accepted his judgment because each member had his day in court. Ultimately, the team's commitment became one of its most powerful strategic assets.

The difficult work of the strategy formulation phase results in a vision that describes an organization's destination and the routes and means for getting there. Tough as it is, it is still only a prelude to the journey itself and the genius required to complete it.

CHAPTER

7

The Bridge to Implementation

The secret is that, number 1, you have to formulate your strategy. The chief executive, every senior executive, has to understand what he or she has to do in the next 3 to 5 years. Without this, it's like kicking the ball around with no goal and no goalkeeper in place. But this is not the end of the job; it is only the beginning. Each day you have to look at "How can I achieve this strategy?" Implementing the strategy becomes your work for the day. Strategy has to be translated into actions—a skill that a lot of executives are lacking.

Number 2, you have to recognize that aligning the strategy and the resulting actions is both a science and an art. The chief executive and his or her team have to be creative in establishing the alignment, and then in creating communication with the people taking those actions to reinforce the strategy.

Third, you have to institute a program whereby progress on those actions is reported in a systematic way. And it has to go beyond reporting to having real two-way communication with those implementing the actions.

The fourth secret is to ensure that everybody in the organization understands your strategy. Just knowing it and seeing it hanging in the hallway isn't enough. Each employee has to understand the answer to "How do I associate my work with the overall company strategy?"

—Alfred W. K. Chan, Managing Director
Hong Kong and China Gas Company Limited

In other words, strategy is easier said than done. Until a strategy has been implemented, it is all thought and no action. A chief executive and his or her top team may be on a well-deserved high after completing the agonizing appraisal of their future direction, but the illusion of having finished is quickly dispelled. There is precious little time to rest.

With a clear destination in mind and navigational aids in hand, the team must pause to ask three things. First, what are the greatest obstacles, many of which we are already aware, that could utterly derail our strategy? Second, what is the general state of our organization's readiness to undertake strategy implementation? And finally, what pitfalls might we encounter as we begin the next phase of our strategic journey?

As Chan suggests, the responsibility for taking these crucial steps lies with the chief executive and his or her top management team. Their commitment must be twofold. The first is a commitment to the strategy itself, especially to significant changes that challenge the status quo. The second is even more demanding: the daily commitment to interpreting and implementing the strategic vision successfully. This commitment to flawless execution is very difficult. The organization's leaders must now become the disciplined protagonists of their strategic intent.

CRITICAL ISSUES

A *critical issue* is a potential or actual problem, decision, or plan that, if left unresolved, would compromise implementation of an enterprise's Driving Force or any other core elements of the strategic profile—competitive advantage, key capabilities, thrust for new business, or return and growth expectations.

Before the strategy team ever meets, most chief executives know of several thorny issues that could undermine the firm's current or likely future strategy. Typical concerns might include avoiding product obsolescence, ensuring the supply of a scarce raw material, maintaining a certain pace in new-product development, or scientific breakthroughs that loom in the distance. Throughout the process of gathering strategic intelligence and articulating the strategic profile, such issues continue to rear their ugly heads. Best-in-class management teams proactively identify and clarify these potential barriers to implementation. They systematically track and analyze these concerns.

If the team is diligent in seeking out these disconnects, it will be well aware of the existing and potential pitfalls—in its assumptions, in the organization's operational management, in its market and product intentions—by the time the vision has been crafted. The top team should confirm these potential threats and gain a sense of their relative priority.

A typical team faces a daunting list of literally hundreds of issues, but not every issue is strategically "Critical." Implementation inevitably includes a host of actions, problems, and hurdles that would require tremendous focus, effort, and creativity to execute or overcome. But here's the litmus test: *Would the inability to resolve this issue jeopardize implementation of the strategy and its related implications? In other words, could it throw the organization irreversibly off course?*

The magnitude of the effort required to resolve it is not the test for qualifying as a critical issue. Rather, the issue must pose a great strategic threat. Critical issues are the showstoppers.

At Towngas, for example, the top team has endorsed a project to pursue the consolidation of purchasing power as they move into the Chinese marketplace. It's an important issue—in fact, it's one of the Key Management Focuses that the team tracks in its meetings. However, the failure to realize a certain margin in that marketplace would not by itself threaten the overall strategy. Therefore, the issue does not qualify as "Critical."

On the other hand, the electronics firm mentioned earlier was facing a show-stopping situation. As much larger and wealthier competitors lured high-caliber radio engineers to better-equipped research facilities at higher salaries, the company's ability to recruit and retain such staff was diminishing rapidly. Initially, based on fierce internal opposition to a competitive pay scheme for these engineers, top management agreed only to upgrade their research facilities. After months of impasse and no improvement in hiring, the task force proposed a separate compensation system, whose higher scale reflected the employment market, the engineers' working conditions, and the limited opportunities for promotion and cross-functional moves. Without the creation and adoption of ideas to attract and retain key workers, the firm would have gone out of business. Indeed, its unwillingness to move quickly to resolve this critical issue did take it to the brink.

Critical issues may have their origins in either the external environment or in the organization and its internal operations. Examples of external issues include the impact of new technology, the merger of two industry rivals that would compromise a firm's ability to compete, or a major adverse and permanent shift in foreign exchange rates.

For example, the human genome project is achieving breakthrough science that could profoundly change the nature of the products and services of pharmaceutical companies. In the foreseeable future, DNA and gene-specific information about each one of us could be stored on an implantable chip so that information could be gathered and catalogued to help predict what preventative treatments we might require. Should such technology go forward, it would have profound strategic implications for most pharmaceutical companies. Would the pharmaceutical giants of the last decade become the chip programmers of the next?

Externally driven critical issues may not be preventable, but they call for thorough analysis of the potential problem, creative alternatives, and a contingent plan to minimize any damaging effect should they occur.

The return and growth expectations of the mobile phone industry have almost certainly been diminished by the far longer than anticipated time frame in which 3G technology has been incubating. A company that has been basing its strategy on the growth originally anticipated in mobile telecoms has had to either shift that strategy, extend its time frame considerably, or seek growth from other sources.

Think of Kennametal's products. These highly engineered components are based on tungsten, a raw material that is currently available primarily in China but not found in many other locations. If for reasons of geopolitical upheaval the supply of tungsten were cut off, Kennametal would have to reconsider the very nature of its products—in this case, its competitive advantage, product differentiation, and superiority. R&D capabilities would immediately need to be deployed to procure or create substitute materials, or the products themselves would be at risk.

Companies have more control over internal issues—a mixed blessing, as these can also be more difficult and painful. A large proportion of critical issues center on a lack of, or weakness in, one or more key capabilities needed to execute strategy. Other potential issues include misalignment of the organizational structure, inadequate buy-in from one or more stakeholder groups, lack of investment capital to support the new strategy, insufficient information about customers or markets, or the relative slowness of product development cycles or time-to-market processes. Any of these may utterly cripple strategic progress.

A critical issue may be of enormous magnitude. We once came to the end of our strategy formulation work with a client team and were having a final session to lay the groundwork for implementation. After a brainstorming exercise, the chief executive took me aside and said, "Convincing our chairman to resign—if he won't, that's the number 1 critical issue that could derail our implementation. Should I raise it this afternoon?" The chairman was a major shareholder and had founded the company 35 years earlier. But the CEO was right to raise this.

To make a painful story short, the chairman didn't resign, but other top executives did over the next year. The company is now a shadow of its former self. In fact, the chairman's dogmatism created several critical issues. He insisted, unlike the rest of the board, on breaking into the U.S. marketplace, ignoring the lack of scale and capabilities for doing so. He was not committed to the idea of "better to be best than first," which required a fundamental shift in the firm's assumptions about research and development and its competitive positioning. He could not accept that the organization's culture needed to evolve to attract and support a new kind of scientist/engineer. He was, indeed, the impenetrable barrier to implementation—and completely out of kilter with the board.

The identification of critical issues is only the first step. In the next chapter, we'll see how they are woven into the overall Strategic Master Project Plan for implementation.

IMPLEMENTATION: IS YOUR ORGANIZATION READY?

In setting strategy, the best chief executives and their teams are already thinking beyond to the question of implementation. Before they create an implementation plan, they are asking questions that help assess the organization's readiness for strategic change. Assuming that your own team has already crafted its strategic vision, how might it respond to the following?

- Do we have a plan in place for our subsidiaries or functional areas to formulate their own strategies as appropriate?

- Is the reporting and operational structure of our company aligned with our strategic intent? How will we track our strategic progress?
- How will the implementation of our product/market matrix priorities affect the balance in our organization?
- Do we have a plan for securing the key processes, capabilities, and skills that we need?
- What changes are needed in our business planning procedures and systems? How will we integrate strategy implementation with our long-range operational planning and budgeting processes?
- Have we built rewards and consequences into our human performance system to encourage strategic behaviors at all levels?
- Do we get the information we need to manage strategically? Are our information technology systems up to the task?
- Does our organization use a common set of rational processes for managing projects, making decisions, solving problems, and anticipating problems and opportunities?
- Do we have a plan for helping our executives and managers learn to think strategically?
- Can we answer, for every stakeholder, "What does this strategy mean for me?" How will those answers be communicated?
- How will we keep the board and the strategy formulation team united as we move toward implementation?
- Overall, do we have the strength and depth we need to implement this strategy?

These are the pivotal questions we'll examine in greater detail in the coming chapters on strategy implementation.

THE WORST PITFALLS

Everybody that's a vice president in our company, and who is responsible for a large portion of business, is totally focused on and dedicated to the execution of that line of business. The hardest thing to get them to do is to think that their line of business is only one part of our overall company— and our overall company strategy. And, you are going to have to give and receive from the other lines of business in order to make us strong as a company. You can't fail to be cooperative in the overall company objectives just because you are trying to maximize your performance within your line of business.

—Jay F. Honeycutt, President
Lockheed Martin's Space Operations

Ultimately, the successful transition from formulation to implementation depends on leadership. As Jay Honeycutt knows so well, the burden is on top executives.

The trap executives face is the potential triumph of operational demands over strategic intent. Too often, and to the company's future peril, operations win out. Far too many leaders yield to operational temptation. They submit to investor demands for short-term returns, quarter-to-quarter evaluations, and an executive reward structure geared to operational performance. Similarly, and to Honeycutt's point, executives find it difficult and distracting to consider the good of the overall company first—that is, to place themselves in a CEO's shoes and take the helicopter view.

Our corporate leaders have always been trained to be operationally proficient, but their strategic education may be seriously lacking. Executive rewards typically follow operational accomplishment; operational goals are measurable and visible, and their attainment brings predictable kudos in the short term. But by its very nature, the success of strategy implementation will be measured over a period of years. Rarely do annual rewards reflect strategic accomplishments that may have been several years in the making, and budgets for performance bonuses are structured accordingly. The weaknesses of the stock-option alternative for rewarding strategic performance are only too evident. Too few executives are privileged to have a leader at the helm who accepts a strategic long view and is building a corporate culture to promote strategic thinking.

The top team carries the onus for strategy implementation. The journey is guaranteed to be a difficult one. As one CEO said (with more accuracy than elegance), the road to strategy implementation is paved not just with good intentions but with "bloody great holes." Here are the most common pitfalls for the team as a whole:

Strategic Inertia—Not Getting Started

More executives than might admit have an inherent resistance to change, or they fail to give it the priority it deserves. Particularly if their own operations are successful, they may be reluctant to rock the boat.

When the Association of International Bond Dealers, whose council is made up of the managing directors of major global bond dealers, set strategy, its intentions were good; however, the members' real commitments were to their own companies. The voluntary nature of the association made it difficult to get implementation off the mark.

A Lack of Stakeholder Commitment to the Vision— Not Having Everyone On Board

If a company's internal and external stakeholders—investors, unions, partners, licensees, capital providers, and local governments, as well as the company's employees—are not on board with the destination and proposed route, the time spent wrangling will rob the company of its agility.

Frequently the strongest blockers of change are middle managers, who admittedly may have the most to lose. For example, the middle-level executives of one global advertising agency rebelled against a new CEO, who eventually capitulated and never brought the team beyond a very early stage of strategy formulation. The "barons" of each specialized subsidiary wouldn't let anyone onto their turf—and the company has since broken up.

Strategic Drift—Not Focusing on the Destination

Sadly, strategic drift often starts with CEO drift. In one company, the CEO simply lost interest once the strategy was formulated. The challenge is especially felt in large, decentralized organizations whose international scope or operational complexity makes strategic discipline all the more difficult. Consider the determination of former Massey-Ferguson CEO Victor Rice and his team: After 9 years of strategy implementation, they still saw the need to stick to the vision and the original tenets of their strategy.

Strategic Dilution—Things Are Moving, But It's Not Clear Who's Driving

If the strategic vision has been formulated through a shared process, the potential for strategic incoherence and inconsistency is minimized. The thrust for growth and new business and the product/market matrix set clear priorities for allocation of resources. The top team may well have experienced unity in its strategy formulation process, and it may have been convinced of that commitment. Yet, when returned to their operational silos, some executives are tempted to ignore directional imperatives and set their own internally competitive priorities for using resources and achieving short-term gain. If several division heads bow to this temptation, the strategy is in serious trouble.

Strategic Isolation—Things May Be Happening, But No One Bothers to Communicate Effectively

Strategy implementation calls for its integration into every aspect of the organization. Consider the Enterprise Model, which we introduced in Chapter 2, as the playing field for strategy. If each one of its internal elements—performance system, key business processes, and so on—is not in sync, there will be troublesome disconnects between strategy and its implementation.

Failure to Understand Progress—Not Knowing Where You Are on the Journey

Without having some means of judging the progress made, the destination will never be reached. Implementation needs milestones, landmarks, and measurable targets for achievement. Without attention to these, the destination may prove elusive.

One CEO commented, "We are pretty good at the operational level. We don't need help with implementation." But he and his team got lost; they forgot to build key indicators of strategic success into their plan for execution.

Initiative Fatigue—Things Are Happening, But Nothing Gets Done

Any organization, especially one that has been struggling, is likely to have taken on a large number of improvement initiatives. Too often, it spins its wheels in the face of project overload. In a cynical environment, the first communications about strategic direction may be welcomed with a yawn and a wink. This too shall pass, one hears.

Impatience—A Demand That Change Take Place Now

Having decided on a vision for the future, many leaders want instant gratification—in other words, immediate implementation. But wise executives know that organizational change requires careful planning, the dedication of appropriate resources—and, above all, time. The "I want it all—now!" culture of many of today's youth just does not work in this domain.

Not Celebrating Success—Failing to Recognize and Reward Progress

We are all human, and a pat on the back for a job well done is a motivating experience. Yet in the urgency of getting the implementation effort underway, this basic tenet of leadership is too frequently ignored. A conscious effort to identify and reward success will pay dividends many times over—especially in the early, and often tense, days and weeks of implementation when the pace quickens and the organization must adjust to a new reality.

The root cause of many of these pervasive, troubling trends is a lack of discipline. The primary discipline required in planning for and actually implementing the strategy is the consistent use and application of a set of project management principles and tools. Companies that have struggled with managing projects in the past can expect strategy to be no different. They may have various difficulties: a lack of project management skills, a lack of discipline in initiating and sustaining the process, or a sloppy approach characterized by competing methodologies and software solutions, but little common ground. Many companies will need to continually reevaluate the relative priorities and conduct an analysis of the optimal portfolio of projects, as we explain in the following chapter.

ON TO IMPLEMENTATION

Over the next several chapters we will explore the remaining three phases of strategy, and how they help an organization avoid or repair these dangerous potholes as the quest begins to bring vision into action.

Our next chapter is on Strategic Master Project Planning. The disciplined project management approach called for in this phase is rewarded many times over. In setting parameters for time, resources, and performance, progress is optimized and measured on visible milestones.

We then address Phase 4 activities: implementing the strategy so that it takes hold at every level of the organization. We will focus on several enablers that our clients deem crucial to the successful execution of a strategic vision: organization structure, complexity, information technology, culture, the performance system, and communication. These must be correctly aligned, or they will doom the strategy itself.

Finally, we will explore Phase 5: monitoring, reviewing, and renewing the vision while the journey is underway.

8

Strategic Master Project Planning

Perhaps the most complicated Strategic Master Project Plan we've seen was done by Lagoven. At the time we worked with them, Lagoven was one of the three state oil companies of Venezuela. Its strategic time frame extended over 10 years, with a plan that eventually encompassed more than 1200 projects. These were grouped into the seven major areas of the business, and they ranged from the exploration of new areas likely to yield oil and gas deposits to the establishment of an appropriate reward system for strategic management. With many thousands of discrete tasks, and many hundreds of employees involved in the execution, the scope was incredible. In fact, it was so vast that we first helped the Lagoven team design a project plan just for creating the Strategic Master Project Plan—an effort that in and of itself took 4 months!

Top teams should know that reluctance or incompetence in crafting the process for implementing strategic change is the single most reliable predictor of its failure.

The scope of this challenge and its potential ramifications can be overwhelming. Implementing strategy calls for an extraordinary shift in the thinking and level of activity of top management. There will be changes to make, often lots of them, and the engine for driving strategic change must be constructed to permeate every corner of the organization. When the approach is undisciplined or ad hoc, this task is downright intimidating.

The key is creating a master plan of strategic projects. To make this task feasible, the job of strategy implementation is built into the work of the entire organization, from its top team to every employee who has a contribution to make to its flawless execution. Without this systematic construct—and the time, resources, and attention dedicated to its success—implementation will fail.

The challenges that lie in creating and executing the Strategic Master Project Plan are more in discipline than in art. Though creativity and judgment will certainly be needed, implementation flounders far too often from a lack of rigor in identifying strategic priorities, insufficient or unrealistic resource allocation, or a lack of discipline in project execution. The organization that fails to overcome these obstacles will see the fruits of its strategy formulation lost in the resulting implementation chaos.

BEYOND ORDINARY PROJECT MANAGEMENT

There is nothing new or mysterious about the importance of project management. Researchers have noted that as much as 70 percent of an organization's activity is project work. The burgeoning interest in the role of project and program management offices, project management software, and project specialists and consultants attests to the demand for agility and responsiveness in today's firms. Regardless of an organization's competitive advantage, its ability to "get stuff done" is of prime importance.

Strategic Master Project Planning includes the elements common to all project management methods: a clear statement of the project's purpose and specific goals and objectives to be met; expectations about project on-time delivery, scheduling, resourcing, cost performance; correct sequencing; and quality/performance standards. However, the Strategic Master Project Plan has the following additional characteristics that distinguish it from day-to-day project management:

- The projects included in the plan—their purpose, objectives, discrete tasks, and measures for success—are driven by the strategic profile itself. The test for inclusion in the Strategic Master Project Plan is whether the project's objectives flow directly from the strategy.

- There typically are a considerable number of diverse projects included in the plan.
- A disciplined prioritization of initiatives is needed to ensure that resources and top management attention are strategically deployed.
- The enterprise-wide adoption of a common project management language and methodology is key; this must be supported by appropriate skill development and rewards for their application.
- The plan requires a disciplined approach to project management methodology, to the structure and roles associated with managing the Strategic Master Project Plan (including a strategy implementation team that reports directly to the top team), and to the monitoring and governance systems that measure its progress.
- The success of the plan ultimately depends on the discipline, commitment, and active support on the part of every member of the organization's top team.

An overview of the process for Strategic Master Project Planning is given in Figure 8-1. The components of the process are discussed in the remainder of this chapter.

WHERE DO STRATEGIC PROJECTS COME FROM?

The purpose of the Strategic Master Project Plan is fourfold: to assess the strategic initiatives that must be undertaken; to integrate into the plan the existing operational projects that continue to be relevant; to identify the projects that must be accomplished first; and to create a system for review and integration of additional projects that keeps their implementation in line with and responsive to the strategic vision.

How does an organization identify such projects? They come from four areas: critical issues, the strategic profile, existing key operational projects that impact the strategy, and from components of the Enterprise Model.

Critical Issues

As discussed in the previous chapter, the first domain lies in the potentially showstopping issues that pose a significant threat to the strategy's success. The projects that address critical issues will be of the highest strategic priority.

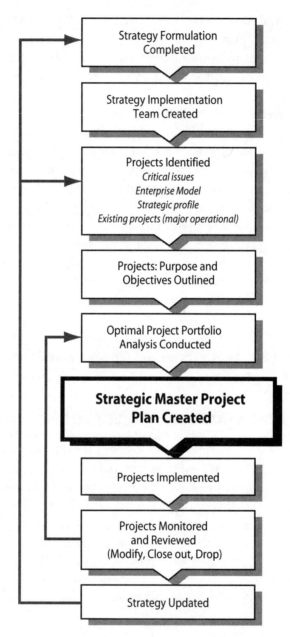

Figure 8-1 Phase 3, Strategic Master Project Planning—An Integrated Process

The Strategic Profile

The strategic profile is fertile ground. The top team must carefully review each of the profile's components to identify the gap between the organization's current state or activities and its ideal at the end of the strategic time frame. These components are the following:

Product/Market Matrix

Products and markets are at the heart of the strategy. Any cell that shows a shift in emphasis and its appropriate activity will constitute a potential strategic project. A typical project statement might be "To enter the Indonesian market and gain a 10 percent market share in widgets by the end of next year" or "To launch a modified form of Product X in all our geographic markets by January 2004." Subprojects for these two examples might be devoted to positioning, branding, promotion, pricing, sales training, or protection of intellectual property.

Competitive Advantage

Based on the strategic profile, an enterprise will either build on its existing sources of competitive advantage, or it will construct a foundation for its future competitive advantage. The projects associated with strengthening or developing competitive advantage generally fall into other categories: key capabilities, product/market emphasis, or the structure and communication aspects of the overall enterprise.

Key Capabilities

A large number of strategic projects typically emerge from the need to fill capability gaps and/or develop people. Their resolution may be quite simple—"Hire 27 additional C++ programmers"—or they may require more creative thinking. Again, key capabilities that are central to the organization's competitive advantage will typically be developed internally; others may be selectively outsourced. One firm we know chose to outsource the administration of human resources, its legal function, and information technology. These were activities that could be better done by best-practice vendors, allowing the top team to focus on those key capabilities where it had the requisite knowledge and skills.

Basic Beliefs

When a top team commits to a project that reinforces implementation of basic beliefs, employees receive a strong and unambiguous message.

For example, a basic belief might state that the company will not do business in countries with poor human rights records. A quick review of the current geographic markets and an Amnesty International report would reveal any disconnects. The result is a statement of a potential project: "To withdraw from the Z-Land market by January 2005."

Strategic Intelligence Gaps

Strategy implementation may require a company to enter unfamiliar product or market territory that is subject to radical external change. Even in familiar markets, there are likely to be gaps in the organization's current knowledge base, as well as the need to anticipate gaps that might arise.

Functional, Divisional, or Business Unit Strategies

A company with a Return/Profit Driving Force will almost certainly need to initiate projects for its subunits to define their own strategies. Organizations with other Driving Forces should also consider the need for these strategic extensions, for example, when the success of a certain division is likely to be profoundly affected by a technological breakthrough or will be linked to a radical shift in the nature of its products or markets. When significant change is called for in the corporate strategy, there is often a requirement for function heads to reassess their own strategy and make the changes needed to support future imperatives.

Potential Mergers, Acquisitions, Alliances, and Joint Ventures

An organization typically undertakes one of these activities in order to (1) obtain products it does not currently have; (2) increase market share significantly or penetrate a new market; or (3) acquire significant capabilities it does not currently have in order to help achieve its strategic goals. Completing an acquisition, alliance, or joint venture project is not a strategy in itself (although many firms position these efforts as such). Rather, it is sometimes the best alternative for obtaining products, markets, or capabilities, and it is thus a key part of successful strategy implementation.

Existing Key Projects

The plain truth is that there are projects—both large and small, relevant to the new strategy or not—already underway in the organization. Although these may have little to do with the strategy per se, they will nonetheless compete for resources and management attention. As a result, they may affect an organization's ability to implement strategy, either by enhancing strategic focus or detracting from it.

Examples of these projects might include the upgrading of telephone equipment and software systems for a call center; installation of an updated production line; or moving headquarters to a new location. Such projects must be reviewed in relation to the Strategic Master Project Plan and prioritized accordingly. Some will be integrated into the plan; others will proceed with little change, or even be discontinued based on resourcing priorities. Without this evaluation, the company will be torn between competing operational and strategic agendas.

The Enterprise Model

Finally, we encourage top teams to use the Enterprise Model as a diagnostic tool for auditing the potential impact of strategy on the organization as a whole. Any gaps that appear will quickly surface here, as the team assesses any remaining gaps or issues that could hinder implementation. Again, the components that comprise the organization's playing field include:

- Leadership
- Business processes
- Goals and measurement
- Human capabilities
- Information and knowledge management
- Organization structure and employee roles
- Culture
- Issue resolution
- The value chain of suppliers, customers, competitors, resource providers, shareholders/parent corporation
- The external environment of governments and communities, the economy, and society at large

Of course, each of these areas suggests a myriad of operational concerns. The question to ask is: "For this component, how do we compare with our strategic ideal?" Many of these gaps will have been apparent during strategy formulation, and some identified as critical issues, yet a review often yields important insights and additional potential projects.

The number and complexity of the projects that constitute the Strategic Master Project Plan will vary greatly from organization to organization. Every plan is unique. However, there are certain core areas—infrastructure, culture, and communication—that are musts, and that will be examined in the next several chapters.

Some projects are relatively simple, although aggressively pursued; others cost virtually nothing, yet are dotted with political landmines due to their complex, cross-functional nature. One company desperately needed to restructure its executive committee to include younger employees with potential and replace those near retirement. This effort cost nothing in tangible resources, but not doing it could have derailed implementation over the strategic time frame. The relative size or cost of a project is not necessarily an indicator of its potential to sink the strategy if left undone.

Drawing on these four sources, the top team gathers a potential pool of projects for the Strategic Master Project Plan. They will range widely in urgency, in importance, and in potential strategic impact.

TOUGH CHOICES: THE OPTIMAL PROJECT PORTFOLIO

One note here before we turn to the Strategic Master Project Plan itself. Unless the organization has unlimited resources—an extremely unlikely scenario—its leaders will have to prioritize. In nearly every case, projects must be prioritized based on the impact and urgency of their results. These projects make up an optimal portfolio that informs the initial sequencing of the overall plan.

The evaluation and ranking of potential projects in the optimal portfolio is similar to the evaluation of alternative Driving Forces, or of potential cells in the product/market matrix. A disciplined decision analysis, weighing the merits of each project against a thorough set of strategic criteria, ensures an actionable outcome. At the same time, an analysis of the resources available to the organization and the resources required for each high-priority project is completed. The combined results of this assessment yield a relative numeric ranking of the entire list of potential projects.

The resulting optimal portfolio shows those projects that fall "above the line," or that can be accomplished within the constraints of currently available resources. This does not mean that a lower-priority project will never see the light of day. Additional projects may be added to the top rung, if the top team chooses to allocate additional resources for the overall plan or redirect priorities. This is also the time for a tough-love look at projects already underway; these may be siphoning off precious resources, have lesser priority than new strategic projects, or even be strategically misaligned (i.e., rapidly moving the organization away from, rather than toward, the new strategy).

As organizational capacity is freed up, the next tranche of projects will be accepted into the portfolio. The optimal portfolio delineates the relative weight of strategic priorities against available resources, and it is therefore the starting point for implementation. As each project is completed, the makeup of the optimal portfolio shifts.

STRATEGIC MASTER PROJECT PLANNING IN ACTION

As the following examples demonstrate, the need for discipline in Strategic Master Project Planning is no different in a skunkworks operation like Crown Greetings than it is in a historically revered organization like the Savoy Group of Hotels. In fact, the life phases of these organizations helped to determine how best to apply these tools, particularly at Crown where every strategic project was undertaken from a ground-zero baseline.

Savoy Group of Hotels: Projects for a Turnaround

In 1997 the top team at the Savoy identified roughly 70 strategic projects to support implementation of its newly formulated strategy and begin a dramatic turnaround in its results.

The Savoy's strategy implementation team grouped these projects into eight major categories: sales and marketing, customer care, business processes, information technology, human resources, finance and control systems, physical product (the hotels and their auxiliary properties), and general management.

Eleven major projects were grouped under the heading of customer care; the purpose of each, briefly stated was:

- To identify current service delivery problems
- To deliver customer care training programs
- To establish competitive monitoring

- To create a guest history via a feedback and monitoring system
- To benchmark customer care programs in other companies
- To establish a customer care team reporting system
- To write performance standards manuals
- To establish a groupwide, common customer guest system
- To gather competitive intelligence through a mystery shopping system
- To introduce quality circles
- To establish rewards for excellent performance

Each of these project statements encompassed a complex project in itself, with many associated subprojects and dozens of discrete tasks.

The overall results achieved by the Savoy? Projects were completed ahead of schedule, with the consequent accelerated achievement of its strategic goals—and financial targets were met 2 years earlier than planned.

Crown Greetings: Starting Off on the Right Foot

At Crown Greetings, CEO Doug Todd was in the privileged position of starting virtually from scratch in pursuing the startup's cell phone greetings business. The Strategic Master Project Plan created by the Crown skunkworks team has been seen as a good learning experience within Hallmark—even though Todd originally had some doubts about his group's ability to make it happen.

The Crown plan included 48 high-level projects and 310 subprojects. Many were focused on creating the foundling company's competitive advantage—most significantly, building and sourcing the technology to support the business. "IT01," as it was known, quickly became all encompassing; the project scope included every facet of technology for the company. A key project was the pursuit and securing of relationships with key partners in the telecom industry—that is, cell phone service providers and manufacturers in each of several targeted geographic markets.

In addition, the Crown plan addressed every aspect of the organization's infrastructure. Separate high-level projects were designed to create key business processes, including product, business, and market development. To support the need for new staff, a set of human resource projects was undertaken to establish consistent processes, policies, procedures, and systems. And on the less glamorous side, one high-level project focused just on setting up the company's offices.

Todd created a position in the startup company with the sole responsibility for tracking progress made on each high-level project plan. What's more, his commitment to creating project management structure and discipline was not a one-time effort. The Crown team developed a set of criteria to identify a project as strategically critical— if it met the criteria, a project was put through rigorous project management planning, and it was closely monitored by management on a monthly basis. In their startup situation, the establishment of a strategy implementation team was inappropriate. The Hallmark parent organization learned much from the "think-big, test-small and scale (or fail) fast" approach embodied in the Crown experience.

Todd was also committed to spreading the skills for project management, decision making, and analysis of potential threats and opportunities through the organization. Workshops enabled senior managers to apply project management skills to key strategic initiatives. In the year that it took to complete this work and the key projects, his managers, says Todd, "delivered something really incredible!"

Todd explains, "The quality of our Strategic Master Project Plan has been the key to our success in launching this business. As the link between formulation and implementation, it was critical that the plan not only be right but be driven at every step by our strategy."

DISCIPLINE IN DRIVING THE PLAN

As Doug Todd demonstrated so tangibly, the top team is responsible for setting the foundation for the best possible execution of the Strategic Master Project Plan. It must choose a systematic process that defines the project management discipline; it must put in place the management structures that will have the authority and responsibility for that discipline; and it must determine how implementation will be measured, controlled, monitored, reviewed, and updated throughout execution.

Systematic Process: The Key to Discipline

It is not our purpose here to examine project management methodologies and their relative benefits. However, the adoption of a project management discipline for strategy implementation must be subject to these criteria:

- A single project management methodology should be used throughout the organization. This common language for projects must be systematic, visible, and transferable to all levels, from the top team to the shop floor. Such a process promotes internal commitment and streamlines communication among project teams as well as project stakeholders.
- The methodology must provide ruthless discipline in the definition of projects, as well as their planning and execution. This secures the clarity of the project's purpose and agreement on its major objectives. These in turn ensure that its scope is finite and that the tasks, resources, and time frame required for its execution are understood. The process also requires creative, transformational thinking. Many enterprises will not have had this experience before and will need to explore every avenue to ensure success.
- The process must provide robust tools and methods for project resource planning, scheduling, and monitoring. Training in these tools must incorporate their hands-on application to real projects, and software applications should support the use of these tools.
- The process must incorporate the human side of project management. In the final analysis, managing projects is about managing people: communicating, negotiating, mentoring, and motivating. Teamwork is no cliché; our experience shows that the number one reason for project failure is the inability of key personnel to work effectively with others.
- The success of implementing any Strategic Master Project Plan lies in the balance individuals can find between their current job requirements and project work. It is up to management to make the time—as well as find the way to reward such efforts and to incorporate them into the formal performance management system.

Building Structure and Defining Roles

Another key to successful implementation: The strategy formulation team must have a management structure in place, along with the systems to support it. Responsibility is best shared between the top team and a committed strategy implementation team.

The top team remains directly involved as the ultimate reviewers of the Strategic Master Project Plan. It monitors the progress of the plan, both through exception reporting on major, individual projects, as well as in weekly or monthly reports on the overall process. It provides continuing guidance on project priorities, re-evaluating their strategic relevance and relative success, and approving the integration of new projects into the plan. The top team is the steward of the organization's resources, allocating both people and funds to priority projects. Finally, its members are the champions of the implementation itself, both as its ultimate sponsors and as the chief communicators. The top team's activities are the focal point for the organization's assessment of strategic progress.

The top team delegates the responsibility for overseeing the execution of the projects themselves to the strategy implementation team. As a first step, this team sets its own charter, including a proposal for communication and interaction with the top team and the rest of the organization, the processes and methods to be used, and the resources it requires. This team also completes the optimal project portfolio analysis. When projects are being executed, the implementation team provides expertise and support to project teams, and in some cases the required training; its members should have expertise in both project management and facilitation. It reports progress on the overall plan and major projects to the top team, and prepares an initial analysis for any additional projects to be considered.

An overview of the ongoing roles for the strategy formulation and implementation teams is provided in Figure 8-2.

The chair of the strategy implementation team should have:

- A strong commitment to and ownership of the strategic vision, forged through membership on the original strategy formulation team and cemented by the respect of his or her peers on that team. This is the role for a seasoned executive, who may well be identified early on in the process as the person who will head implementation efforts.
- Experience in managing major projects, and a deep appreciation of the scope of major projects from "soup to nuts."

Strategy Formulation Team
Development of strategic criteria for project assessment
Review, sign off, and resource commitment
Quarterly top management review of projects
Projects integrated into long-range planning and operational budgets
Overall strategy monitored, reviewed, and updated

Strategy Implementation Team
Initial project definition
Recommendations: Priority projects
Analysis of available resources
Detailed project planning
Project management methodology
Skills and training
Ongoing evaluation/recommendations
Project Support Office
Support for project teams
Facilitation support
Project monitoring

Figure 8-2   Phase 3, Strategic Master Project Planning: Roles and Responsibilities

- Broad exposure to all facets of the business and a holistic understanding of the organization.
- A direct reporting relationship to the chief executive.
- Excellent people skills: the ability to work with teams, to communicate, negotiate, build relationships, confront others, and say no.
- Support for giving up everyday job responsibilities, so that attention may be totally devoted to strategy implementation.
- The discipline to not only adhere to but promote the chosen project methodology and processes.

If the master plan is especially complex, a formal project support office may be created to provide day-to-day monitoring, training, and expertise. It acts as a "center of competence" to assist project teams.

The size and nature of the implementation team, and of the project support office, if needed, depends on the scope of the implementation and the resources available. The top team must be realistic. For example, one Swiss company has recently committed a single person *half-time* to be responsible for $1 billion plus in project work—a level of commitment that is likely doomed to failure. Project support offices vary, ranging from 2 members to 12; in an example of the latter, one individual was dedicated simply to the recruitment of resources when a project ran short; another, to examining and resolving all cross-project dependencies. There is no magic formula, and organizations can expect these structures to change as implementation unfolds.

Finally, project teams are formed for the execution of individual projects. Project roles—project manager, sponsor, resources, and stakeholder—are clearly identified. Every participant in implementation, from the top team to individual project resources, must understand his or her responsibilities for managing, reviewing, and executing projects.

Putting "Teeth" into the Plan: Monitor and Manage

The top team must also secure an ongoing approach to monitoring and managing the success of the overall Strategic Master Project Plan.

Effective systems must be created by the strategy implementation team for reporting progress on all major projects and significant exceptions to top management. In the early stages, this reporting may occur at weekly intervals; eventually, monthly reporting may suffice. The top team retains its responsibilities throughout implementation. We will discuss the management, review, and updating of strategy in greater detail in Chapter 12.

The optimal portfolio of projects must be reviewed regularly by the top team in order to limit project proliferation. With the same discipline applied to the initial selection, projects that are in the pipeline, as well as new projects suggested by feedback on the progress of the plan, are re-evaluated against the whole.

The top team also must consciously manage employee behavior to include rewards for performance on projects and behaviors in support of the strategy. We will look more closely at the importance of such a system in our chapter on strategic culture.

DRIVING THE PLAN: THE ART OF LEADERSHIP

We estimate that the ratio of strategies formulated to those completely and flawlessly implemented is roughly 10 to 1. Many of these formulated strategies would have succeeded had efforts to implement them been guided by the creation and application of a Strategic Master Project Plan.

As the ultimate reviewers and champions, the top team must be aware of the potential roadblocks to building a strong master project

plan and avoid them or minimize their impact. If yours is a typical organization, you'll have encountered some or all of these:

- Failure to adhere to a systematic, visible process for prioritizing
  and planning strategic projects. The ability to say no—to sidestep
  the temptation to do too much or to add personal favorites that
  lack strategic relevance—is the only defense against project proliferation, a certain death knell for implementation.
- Wishy-washy commitment by senior managers to the silo-
  busting nature of a coherent strategy implementation, and an unwillingness to subject their own areas to top management scrutiny.
- Lack of clarity in defining the roles of the strategy implementation team and the project support office, so that they are unable
  to support project efforts, because they are too busy policing and
  enforcing compliance.
- Lack of commitment to dedicating the appropriate resources
  to priority projects, with appropriate coverage for day-to-day
  responsibilities. Too often, there are unrealistic expectations for
  project work, and project teams find their resources exhausted
  and their people overwhelmed. Often, a performance system
  that rewards and recognizes only operational successes, rather than
  the all-important work of strategy implementation, compounds
  the problem.
- Omission of a rigorous analysis of potential problems and opportunities within individual project plans as well as the overall
  plan. Such an analysis should include plans for action to avoid
  or minimize anticipated problems, and to identify and capitalize
  on opportunities that appear on the horizon.
- Insufficient discipline in monitoring the progress of the plan,
  particularly on the part of the top team.

IN SUMMARY

To our knowledge, no single project in the history of the world has
managed to avoid Murphy's law. The likelihood that an entire Strategic
Master Project Plan will meet its time, cost, and performance expectations without a hitch is zero. When the inevitable exceptions and varia-
tions are reported, the top team must seek out and remedy the causes.

When progress is habitually below expectations, it may be forced to ask, "Is this strategy realistic, or are we below par in its execution?"

Like setting strategy, we suspect that implementation may never be complete. In the best of all possible worlds, implementation is woven into the fabric of the organization, and it is responsive to the shifting needs of a strategy that is also under constant review.

The rate of change in nearly every industry sector will continue to accelerate. The chief executive who seeks to keep a firm but responsive hand on the tiller will be greatly aided through the application of project management disciplines to strategy implementation.

The Strategic Master Project Plan is the most powerful—and nimble—tool available to drive the business forward. It enables a top team to respond dramatically, with the full weight of its financial and human resources, to the pivotal events that determine its strategic efficacy. The task is formidable in the creativity, analysis, even stamina required, but the alternative is unacceptable. As in the formulation of the strategy itself, the organization that fails to bring discipline to bear will find itself adrift all too soon.

Implementation: Aligning the Infrastructure

A well-known but poorly performing consumer goods enterprise had neglected its strategic direction for too long, prompting its board to recruit a new chief executive. The firm was dysfunctional; subsidiaries, functions, and individuals all played their own tunes. It lacked both an effective organization structure and a strategically relevant information base. Many of the products and customers in its vast array were unprofitable; it was too complex. Over his first 2 years with the firm, the new CEO fought to clarify the firm's vision and to align these infrastructure elements with it. Now he is able to assure its stakeholders that the ingredients for future success are in place.

Even the best of Strategic Master Project Plans will take a business into uncharted territory. Like the company above, in which several internal factors had a critical effect on strategy implementation, the top team's task is not finished just because a plan is in place.

The fourth of our strategic phases, strategy implementation, is clearly a matter of "walking the talk." And make no mistake, if the glamour is in formulating strategy, the genius is in its implementation.

While every Strategic Master Project Plan differs, each will generally address several common areas. These are so important that they must be reviewed and, when necessary, corrected to ensure alignment with the strategic intent. These efforts become major strategic projects in their own right; improperly aligned, each of these areas could seriously hinder implementation.

In this chapter, we examine three of these crucial areas: organization structure; strategic information management; and complexity, particularly with respect to the relationship between products, customers, and profitability.

In the next two chapters, we will look at two equally important keys to successful implementation: (1) culture and its expression through the management of human performance and, (2) communicating the strategy. Each of these is linked to the internal components of the Enterprise Model presented in Chapter 2, reflecting the organic nature of strategy implementation.

Chief executives and their top teams may fall prey to three common—and costly—misconceptions about infrastructure:

- Formulating a strategy calls for an automatic restructuring of the organization.
- Gathering and reporting information has little relevance for strategy implementation.
- An organization can pursue a new strategy while continuing with every current activity.

Each of these has serious implications for implementation.

CREATING THE OPTIMAL ORGANIZATIONAL STRUCTURE

Since restructuring is often seen as a panacea for an underachieving organization, a CEO may have tried it before setting strategy, hoping a structure fix would resolve directional difficulties. Or the CEO may simply assume that a new strategy will call for a restructuring project. In either case, the attempted remedy ignores the relationship between strategy and structure. Why is restructuring such a seductive trap?

Unfortunately, CEOs are tempted to pull organizational strings when results are not what they should be, when a competitor makes a bold move, or even when the company has a breakthrough. With authority and responsibility squarely on their shoulders, CEOs may choose restructuring initiatives to make a sweeping statement about their ability to lead.

Restructuring may also seem easier than strategy. Rightly or not, a CEO and the top team may perceive that strategy formulation will open a formidable "can of worms," where a deft reorganization might remedy short-term operational or profitability issues. Yet in practice, repetitive and/or inappropriate restructuring and shifts in top management are often the symptoms of a poorly defined strategy. In fact, such habitual adjustments may lead to a degradation of corporate and employee performance, which tempts managers to shift again, thus beginning a destructive cycle of change. Such frequent changes are no substitute for a thorough strategy review. Worst of all, restructuring is often done to accommodate key individuals, rather than the exigencies of the business.

Finally, a focus on restructuring appeals to top management's need for clarity, order, and hierarchy. Yet the formal organization structure rarely describes how work actually gets done.

Whenever a strategy has been formulated, a company's structure should be examined to ensure that it promotes implementation. If it does, then it should be left alone. If it inhibits implementation, then restructuring is justified. For example, a metal fabrication company decided that its Products Offered Driving Force should take the business into new geographic markets. These new markets were largely international, but the existing structure did not support global sales, purchasing, or distribution. The need for change was clear.

Default structures are often based on geography or types of manufacturing activities. Yet the top team must look first to the strategic vision for guidance. If the Driving Force is Products Offered, for example, an organization will almost certainly consider a structure that reflects its major product categories; it might also consider organizing by market if that structure will fuel growth.

The product/market matrix, key capabilities, and core business processes to support the strategy may yield important clues to an optimal structure, as we will see later. Selecting a structure should be undertaken with the same rigor as choosing a Driving Force. Most importantly, the selection criteria must be rooted in the strategic vision if the structure is to successfully support implementation.

The following criteria were developed by a European entity that straddles the line between private and government activity. Its top team selected a structure based on these criteria:

- Brings better balance in regional development
- Strengthens the influence we have on government decision making
- Ensures targeted customer groups meet our goals for their contribution to the national economy
- Focuses the scope of our services on the needs of our key customers
- Builds stronger links between headquarters, our international operations, and our domestic regional staff at the point of customer interface
- Enables clear goals to be set and drives effective performance toward those goals
- Strengthens the HR, business development, and knowledge of management functions
- Incurs no added cost
- Uses current staff and their skills wherever possible
- Allows for individuals to grow into new jobs with new skills
- Emphasizes our new business focus and requirements for growth
- Upgrades the planning function
- Places key responsibility for delivery with divisional managers
- Facilitates optimum collaboration between regions, divisions, and functions

These objectives were derived from strategic goals ("new business focus and growth") and from concerns for operations and processes ("upgrades the planning function"). This team evaluated several alternatives, only one of which was to dismantle the current structure and replace it with a new one.

Jeff Warren, chief executive of the Bristol and West Bank, tells this story of the restructuring requirements dictated by his firm's recently updated strategy, which called for entry into "advice-based financial services":

A key issue arose in the course of our strategy formulation discussions that indicated a need for restructuring. We accepted the concept of a new product category called "[financial] advice," which we then fit into the framework of our product/market matrix.

Our definition of "advice" as a new-product area required us to make our first move through acquiring an entirely separate business. Chase De Vere was the first of our three acquisitions; it was self-standing, had its own culture, its own way of doing things, its own functionalities—and that posed an immediate challenge to our own structure. The Bristol and West Bank had always been a substantially integrated organization, and we felt we couldn't justify behaving in one fashion in the selling of mortgages and savings, our core business, and another way in the selling of "advice." Our dilemma was whether to take away the autonomy of Chase de Vere to bring it into the integrated Bristol and West structure or to split our existing businesses and build them along the autonomous Chase model.

Based on the Products Offered Driving Force we had adopted, we suspected that our structure should be driven by the organization's product makeup. We had difficult choices to make in designing our business units and their product areas. One of our primary criteria was that we would try to capitalize on synergy between the products in a single business unit. We knew we were headed toward building independent business units with a strong product focus, and we wanted to ensure that the structure did not force people to fight their way across business unit barriers in order to generate product synergies.

There is still work that needs to be done, but we've crashed through quite a lot of thinking on exactly what the center is, what belongs there and why, and what the role of the business unit is. For us, the strategy came first, and the structure flowed out of the strategy.

Several lessons are clear from the experiences of Warren and his team. First, they turned to the strategy, specifically the Driving Force, to find a rational basis for structure—in this case, a synergy among products within business units. Second, the acquisition of a new entity was aligned with the thrust for new business, and it provided both market access and key capabilities in support of the strategy. Third, the team knew that structure should flow from strategy, rather than the reverse. Its reason for changing the structure was to pave the way for implementation.

The structure issue is often complicated by mergers and acquisitions. One U.K. consumer products business consisted of the original enterprise along with four other acquired companies, each with its own infrastructure, culture, and, indeed, strategy. Before it could reasonably expect its U.K. operations to implement the parent company's global strategy effectively, the business needed to create a single unified entity. Key to the design were the core business processes needed to execute the strategy—in this case, product development and business development. Of course there were other criteria for the structure—for example, consolidation of manufacturing—but these were all of lesser importance than those that related to the alignment with core processes.

When top teams consider the possible restructuring of an organization for strategic reasons, they should remember that a formal structure of reporting relationships and decision-making hierarchies does not necessarily describe *how* work gets done. Some organizations find a viable alternative in a structure designed around core business processes. For example, new-product development is often one of a Markets Served–driven company's core processes, and it is always closely linked to its strategy. Depending on the strategic profile, other companies might find that their route-to-market processes are central, and thus their logistics and distribution capabilities might drive an optimal structure.

Business processes are "the steps that convert inputs to outputs."[1] As shown in the Enterprise Model, processes define how work is done as it flows through an organization's structure of formal relationships and approved departmental budgets. Strategy—which defines *what* work should be done rather than *how* work should be done—helps the top team determine:

- Which processes should be in place
- Which processes should have priority
- Which capabilities are needed to support these processes

The answers to these questions will yield critical clues to the structure that will best serve the strategy and the organization's future direction.

CREATING AND MANAGING
STRATEGIC INFORMATION

To formulate strategy and draw up the Strategic Master Project Plan requires relevant information. Every leadership team expects its organization's capacity for gathering, storing, retrieving, and synthesizing information to play a crucial role in its success. Yet it risks strategic failure if it does not build the development, analysis, and dissemination of strategically critical information into its implementation plan.

Several pitfalls await. The most common is the tendency to become weighed down in operational data. Such data are always readily available. Every day, projected, actual, and historical numbers are crunched, configured, and reported for every aspect of the business: costs, production, sales, marketing, and inventory—every area important in its own right but not necessarily strategically relevant. The distraction of this day-to-day data flow can leave little time for strategic support.

At worst, the failure to acquire and evaluate strategically relevant information is a barrier to strategy implementation. If information is cumbersome, poorly presented, overwhelming, or only vaguely relevant, it can sideline entire project and management teams with a mass of irrelevant data. And of course, any company runs the risk of encountering a competitor who plays the information card correctly to its competitive advantage.

Such an advantage is gained when information is optimized to support strategic activities. Given an understanding of the strategy, the IT function must play a critical role in meeting the need for strategic information, as well as the information normally required for operational, financial, and planning purposes.

Ideally, this focus begins in the earliest phase of the strategy process. The emphasis of these tasks shifts as progress is made:

- In Phase 1, the strategy formulation team may well require support for obtaining superior access to data and research for strategic intelligence gathering.
- In Phase 2, strategy formulation, the team may need to call on technical resources to generate scenarios for relative product/market emphasis and potential return/profit configurations.

- In Phase 3, software capabilities can ease the task of generating the Strategic Master Project Plan. The adept application of such tools will lay the foundation for generating mission-critical information as the plan is implemented and managed.
- Throughout strategy implementation and its ongoing monitoring and review, the strategy implementation team, project teams, and project support staff must acquire, analyze, and effectively communicate information on the progress of individual projects, the overall plan, and the Key Indicators of Strategic Success.
- Based on the key trends identified in the initial environmental assessment (economic, political, demographic, and competitive), the top team must allocate resources to gather, sift, and analyze data for feeding back strategically relevant information to the ongoing strategy review and update process.

The Driving Force of an organization will help determine its most important strategic information needs. For example, the Royal Mail's choice of a Method of Distribution Driving Force had important implications for its IT function, which was redirected toward gathering data on distribution performance. For example, internal measures of "letters delivered next day" were put in place; external intelligence gathering focused on trends in other communication media and the volume of traffic distributed by alternative means.

The implications of the Hallmark International strategy for its information requirements were related to its Products Offered Driving Force and its competitive advantage of "understanding and touching the consumer emotionally." This competitive advantage helped management shift its focus from its customers (existing retail outlets) to its end users (the senders and receivers of its greetings products). Thus, the data most relevant to the strategy were those on consumer habits and buying motives for greeting others, many of them driven by local culture. The nature of the reports and analysis therefore changed radically—and supported a more compelling relationship with its retail customers as well.

The implications of other Driving Forces are easily inferred. An organization driven by Return/Profit will likely find its most useful information in sophisticated profit analyses. A company with a Markets Served Driving Force is likely to need data on the demographics and related trends of its current consumer franchise, seeking to understand what other needs it might meet.

The information glut shows no sign of abating. Winning organizations will harness their people, time, and IT capabilities to ensure that the strategic dimension of information comes first.

REDUCING COMPLEXITY

No CEO worth his or her salt would advocate greater complexity for an organization, yet complexity is often bred at the very top level of management. There is dire temptation to be all things to all people—and therefore supply every possible customer or market with every imaginable product permitted within its strategic framework. Quite simply, no chief executive likes to say no, and few senior executives willingly relinquish their personal product or market favorites.

Every strategy team has a duty to scrutinize the complexity that most likely lurks in its organization. Left unattended, it can cripple strategy implementation.

Complexity in the Supply Chain

In the U.K. division of a major international stationery supplier, excessive product proliferation based on every conceivable consumer whim resulted in a horrendous complexity that was incompatible with its new strategic imperatives. In this division alone, tens of thousands of SKUs and thousands of customers were on the books. Pencils of every size and shape, for example, with and without erasers, in dozens of different shades and tints, were available in a multitude of package sizes. The firm routinely accepted orders for its most obscure items in miniscule quantities, even providing overnight delivery. Inevitably, the typical customer placed these offbeat orders perhaps twice a year—and bought the bulk of its supplies from another firm. The firm lost money on every such order, but in spite of this, it continued the practice for years.

While this firm was demonstrably complex in its supply chain—vendors, customers, and products—it did not act until it realized that it would either go out of business or be sold. The parent would not tolerate the firm's existing strategy, given its intolerable level of profit and the impossibility of implementing that strategy successfully.

Why do companies and their top teams fail to recognize how such practices deplete the organization's resources and profits? Lack of strategic discipline is only part of the answer. Many companies are burdened with standard cost accounting that fails to reflect the true costs associated with low-volume activities.

An automobile specialty manufacturing plant in Germany owned by Corning, Inc. responded to rising demand by increasing its production to record levels. When the bottom fell out of the market and demand fell by 30 percent in a single month, the team at U.S. headquarters threatened to shut down or sell the plant if management could not reverse the downward spiral in volume and profitability.

At the urging of our colleagues George Elliott and Vern Luepker, plant management reworked its cost reporting to tie variable costs—training, overtime, downtime, equipment modifications—directly to specific products, rather than allocating them across product lines without regard to volume. With this redistribution, the disparities in product costs quickly became clear. On a standard cost basis, one low-volume, hard-to-manufacture product appeared to be 20 percent more costly than a high-volume, easy-to-manufacture product. When cost data were restructured to reflect the true allocation of product costs, the variance was shown to be 500,000 percent! One critical factor: the time engineers spent supervising production of the low-volume product.

Such analysis has borne out Elliott and Luepker's "Rule of 50/5." The viability of this principle has been confirmed as we've helped clients analyze their product and market complexity, often in conjunction with their strategic efforts. Like the well-known Pareto rule of 80/20, the Rule of 50/5 describes the phenomenon of organizational complexity. The top 5 percent of the number of products sold in a given company typically account for at least 50 percent of the revenue generated. Similarly, the top 5 percent of a company's customers typically account for at least 50 percent of its revenue. Likewise, the bottom 50 percent of many organizations' customers will account for only 5 percent of revenues.

Figure 9-1 is a chart of one company's products ranked according to total sales dollars. The report lists each product, the units sold, revenue by unit, accumulated revenue, and the percentage of total sales represented. This is only the first page of the data that illustrate the Rule of 50/5. Again, according to the Rule roughly 50 percent of the sales revenue is generated by the top 5 percent of the number of products (roughly 50 of 1011 total products). The report reveals that in fact the top 38 products—just 3.8 percent of the total number of products—account for half the revenue. The top 8 products—less than 1 percent of the total number—account for roughly 20 percent of total revenue.

The remainder of this 30-page report demonstrates the corollary to this rule dramatically—that is, that the lower 50 percent of the total number of products generate only 5 percent of the company's revenue. In fact, the remaining pages, not shown in this excerpt, show that the bottom 50 percent (507 products) account for a miniscule 0.7 percent of total revenue!

| | | Products Ranked by Sales | | | |
Product Rank	Units	Sales $	Accum. Sales $	% Total Sales	Accum. % Total Sales
1	114,390	2,956,357	2,956,357	4.3%	4.3%
2	80,277	2,012,178	4,968,534	2.9%	7.2%
3	139,958	1,622,169	6,590,703	2.4%	9.6%
4	63,277	1,602,800	8,193,503	2.3%	11.9%
5	239,577	1,528,507	9,722,010	2.2%	14.2%
6	175,763	1,297,122	11,019,133	1.9%	16.1%
7	49,450	1,224,486	12,243,619	1.8%	17.8%
8	33,151	1,214,443	13,458,061	1.8%	19.6%
9	83,786	1,061,569	14,519,630	1.5%	21.2%
10	63,044	1,049,981	15,569,611	1.5%	22.7%
11	39,046	1,046,869	16,616,481	1.5%	24.2%
12	39,320	1,041,058	17,657,538	1.5%	25.7%
13	59,064	1,007,261	18,664,799	1.5%	27.2%
14	57,190	921,143	19,585,942	1.3%	28.5%
15	35,884	888,527	20,474,469	1.3%	29.8%
16	37,268	849,095	21,323,564	1.2%	31.1%
17	34,562	805,840	22,129,404	1.2%	32.2%
18	51,416	778,587	22,907,991	1.1%	33.4%
19	92,965	768,870	23,676,861	1.1%	34.5%
20	41,664	666,624	24,343,485	1.0%	35.5%
21	56,544	645,227	24,988,711	0.9%	36.4%
22	48,695	636,619	25,625,330	0.9%	37.3%
23	105,445	617,837	26,243,167	0.9%	38.3%
24	35,002	616,289	26,859,457	0.9%	39.1%
25	26,094	603,226	27,462,683	0.9%	40.0%
26	40,468	584,825	28,047,508	0.9%	40.9%
27	139,167	578,798	28,626,306	0.8%	41.7%
28	107,527	560,254	29,186,559	0.8%	42.5%
29	60,672	556,392	29,742,952	0.8%	43.3%
30	101,202	555,588	30,298,540	0.8%	44.1%
31	74,784	541,059	30,839,599	0.8%	44.9%
32	82,619	539,670	31,379,269	0.8%	45.7%
33	39,538	533,763	31,913,032	0.8%	46.5%
34	22,821	516,653	32,429,685	0.8%	47.3%
35	34,594	501,440	32,931,125	0.7%	48.0%
36	102,820	493,248	33,424,373	0.7%	48.7%
37	66,846	476,015	33,900,388	0.7%	49.4%
38	**32,900**	**458,867**	**34,359,255**	**0.7%**	**50.1%**

Total Sales: $68m
Total Products: 1011

Top 50% sales
38/1011 products
(3.8%)

Bottom 50% sales
973/1011 products
(96.2%)

Figure 9-1 Demonstrating the Rule of 50/5

Further analyses showed similar trends across all brands in this company. And the profiles of sales by customer showed that, as with our stationery supplier, low-volume products tended to be purchased by low-volume customers.

These companies are not alone in failing to address complexity caused by the sheer number and characteristics of the products and markets currently pursued and proposed for the future. No organization can hope to implement its strategy without tackling the complexity trap.

Another kind of complexity is equally insidious—that of the organization's internal activities and business processes.

Consider, for example, the processing of an insurance claim. One company we worked with estimated that a typical claim passed through 15 hands before a final determination of the company's response was made.

A common route for reducing complexity in business processes is to identify those that are candidates for outsourcing. But to reduce complexity of any kind, the top team must act in concert with the strategy to ensure that the difficult choices to be made will strengthen rather than endanger its implementation.

Complexity and Strategy

The evaluation of complexity in products and markets begins long before implementation. The very act of integrating current products and customers into a product/market matrix that reflects the company's Driving Force and its thrust for growth and new business raises vital questions.

Initiatives to reduce complexity must reflect the scope, emphasis, and financial mix of the product/market matrix. When a team chooses to add new products and markets to the mix, it is inevitably adding complexity. Yet the need to achieve revenue, profits, and growth from new areas of activity will often supercede the requirements for operational streamlining. Whatever the exact relationship between specific products or customers and the revenue and profits they generate, a thorough audit of the product/market matrix often reveals disparities between the emphasis a segment requires and the financial return generated.

Of course, complexity reduction may be operationally appropriate in any case, although organizations must avoid cutting into strategic muscle and bone. Cross-correlated analyses (like the preceding example) on sales, customers, profits, costs of production, and other factors will quickly reveal those existing product and customer activities that are eating away at the bottom line.

This information should inform the completion of the product/market matrix, so that specific cells are identified for a lower degree of emphasis—or even exclusion. Revenue may be sacrificed, but the gains almost always outweigh the revenue hit.

In any case, the process is iterative. The top team must look for balance between the requirements of the strategic vision and a tolerable degree of product and market complexity. Smart organizations will capitalize on the savings realized through reducing complexity by redirecting resources to new strategic imperatives. Most critical is the team's commitment to staying focused on the strategic vision and avoiding tempting diversions that dilute attention to the strategic musts.

LOOKING AHEAD

These three indicators of the health of the organization's infrastructure—its structure, its capabilities for gathering and analyzing strategic information, and its complexity—must be scrutinized. Each must be brought into alignment with the strategy over the course of the strategic time frame, and any immediate barriers to the success of implementation must be removed. These key implementation areas bridge strategy into the operational realm, with the task of making it a reality.

In the next chapter, we turn to the human side of strategy implementation: the corporate culture, as well as the system for managing performance and rewards to encourage strategically aligned behaviors.

10

Implementation: Aligning Strategy, Culture, and Performance

To offer a stream of new products and services to Towngas's strong customer franchise, creative and forward thinking among our employees was a must. We needed a new cultural framework in order for the strategic vision to take hold. We had to prepare people mentally to be able to accept challenges. After all, Towngas is more than 135 years old. It has a sense of culture that is related directly to Hong Kong and to our gas business only. After 3 years, we have begun to unravel that status quo.

—Alfred W. K. Chan, Managing Director
Hong Kong and China Gas Company Limited

THE "SOFT SIDE" AND BEYOND

Too many chief executives make the mistake of leaving the human, or "soft," side of the management equation to the human resource function. Even with the clearest of strategies and the soundest of infrastructures, a company's strategic vision will remain just that unless it is supported by an organization's cultural underpinnings, day-to-day decision making, behaviors, and performance.

Addressing the soft side of implementation is not optional. Forget half-hearted attempts at corporate bonding or backwoods adventures to bring teams together; they don't add much value. There is a direct line-of-sight from strategy to culture to performance, and then to business results. To ignore the human side of strategic change is to jeopardize the chances of achieving business and financial goals.

The top team of a well-known global advertising agency reviewed its strategy and decided to shift the focus away from selling lots of new, relatively small projects to a large number of accounts. Instead, it sought to exploit its relationships with senior executives in a small number of multinational clients by promoting significantly larger and more complex projects, thereby increasing the revenue yield and extending the half-life of each account.

Not surprisingly, the communication of this change was executed superbly in their many offices around the world. The new strategy was clear and viable, and employees saw top management's total commitment to it.

There was an initial burst of enthusiasm for the new direction, but 18 months later, not much had changed. The new strategy was ignored in the marketplace. Account managers did not focus on the new paradigm. Projects remained small, and the number of clients continued to grow. Executives on the top team became frustrated and planned to replace a large number of account managers. While their frustration was understandable, it was misdirected.

The organization had long been characterized by a lone-ranger culture. It did not reinforce the new strategy at a regional or individual level. Furthermore, the way it managed and rewarded the performance of key employees did not support the new strategy. Business developers continued to "cherry pick" rather than spend the time and effort building client relationships for larger projects.

Until the organization addressed the misalignment of its strategy, culture, and performance, it continued to flounder.

So what then is culture? We define it as "the combined effect of behaviors, values, heritage, thinking, and relationships and the way these are embedded in an organization and its performance."[1] It is an unmistakably positive force when it is in alignment with the strategy and an organization's people management. When misaligned, however, it can be disruptive and a serious barrier to implementation.

Anyone who has had the privilege of knowing the large number of companies that we do can attest that each one's unique culture is seen and felt as soon as you enter its doors. But not every element of culture is easily identified or understood. Culture inevitably includes both manifest components—values and behaviors that are intentionally or explicitly expressed—as well as latent elements that are often hidden and part of the organization's "subconscious."

To implement strategy effectively, leadership must address both of these, with special attention to those premises that have remained unchallenged over the course of many years. Making the elements of culture visible and explaining why they are important in achieving a firm's goals are crucial.

This underscores the importance of basic beliefs to the strategy formulation process. They are a key input for setting strategy. A company's beliefs about quality, customer relationships, product leadership, growth, and the like have a direct effect on the selection and definition of the Driving Force, the value it brings to customers, and the capabilities with which it delivers that value. Once the strategy is set, the question becomes: How do we use our basic beliefs to facilitate implementation?

Basic beliefs are a necessary but insufficient prerequisite for aligning culture with strategy and performance. Leadership is also vital. Executives who have successfully defined and shaped a strategic culture have a high degree of sensitivity and understanding of their corporations. They have a talent for uncovering latent values and norms that are expressed, and that have an almost gravitational pull on decision making and behavior.

Where do you look for clues about culture? *One place to look is in the past.* The myths, legends, and stories about an organization constitute the lore of its culture; as they are shared, disseminated, and retold, they become powerful symbols. Accurate or not, strategically meaningful or not, the lessons learned through such tales are much more than idle water-cooler talk. They may define the very core of a culture.

During the period 1994 through 1997, the leaders of the Labour Party machine were well aware of the need to instill different cultural norms to support the new strategy. Its defeats in four successive general elections had become the subject of legends—and had demoralized the party at every level—in Parliament, at headquarters, and with members up and down the country.

The power of this history was reflected in the pervasive short-hand of corridor conversations: The party had experienced "glorious defeat," "fought the best campaign," claimed that "winning isn't every-thing," and even that "it might be better to be in the opposition at present." Reversing this thinking was no simple matter of organization structure or new management techniques. The new strategic culture called for ditching these assumptions and creating a new set of stories and symbols around victory, power, confidence, and success, rather than glorious failure.

Thus, beginning with members of the party leadership's manage-ment team, the party examined its myths at every level, and eventually created a new language that took hold in every crevice of the political leadership through disciplined role modeling. This led in part to the victory in the 1997 election.

As the general election of 2001 neared, talk was of "a second straight victory," "outdoing our performance of 1997," and "becoming the natural party of government"—simple stories that helped build a totally different, and strategically aligned, culture.

Look also to where your organization spends its time. For example, the average executive spends many hours per week in meetings. Take this test: Think back to the last 10 meetings you attended. How much agenda time was devoted to discussing business strategy? How many action items coming from those meetings dealt with implementing some key element of that strategy or were aimed at testing its underly-ing assumptions?

If your organization is like many others, your meetings are likely to focus on past operational and financial results and issues. This is one telltale sign that your culture may not support your future strategy.

Look at your organization's cultural artifacts. They are everywhere. To what extent is strategic culture embedded in the information that is provided to executives? What cultural messages are present in business processes, in policy manuals and planning documents, in internal newsletters and hiring profiles? Each of these artifacts must be consis-tent with the kind of culture to which your company aspires. If, for example, the strategy calls for collaborative team selling, yet the hiring objectives include only measures of outstanding solo achievements, the culture will remain out of sync.

Look at your physical working environment; it is a culture carrier that may either support or impede strategy implementation. At Crown Greetings, Doug Todd has had to walk a fine line between nurturing the entrepreneurial spirit of the skunkworks culture of early days and laying the foundation for ongoing strategic discipline as the organization matures into a successful business. He leads an extraordinary mix of young, creative thinkers and traditional managers steeped in Hallmark traditions. Todd has chosen to make management style and behavior as visible as possible, even insisting that Crown's offices include virtually no walls. Operating "in public" at all times has forced his leaders to model leadership that balances creative thinking with strategic discipline. And he expects that discipline itself will continue to nurture even more creativity.

Communication with external audiences—customers, investors, suppliers, media, and the general public—often speaks volumes about a company's culture. Are the messages delivered to these groups strategically aligned? The Body Shop's beauty products reflect a corporate belief in environmental protection. Its products are now offered globally with an emphatically self-conscious appeal to customers who like the image of environmental responsibility and want to contribute to it. This critical marketing message is built around a culture shared between customers and Body Shop employees. Customers could surely find products of higher quality or lower cost, but they choose not to; similarly, employees are likely to be recruited with the promise of joining an organization with politically correct attitudes and actions. We'll look more closely at the issue of communication in the following chapter.

Forces outside your organization may leave cultural residues that impact your strategy implementation effort. Some CEOs question whether the nature of their particular culture might be determined partially by the macro-sector in which they operate—for example, in a certain industry, or government, or not-for-profit. They wonder whether a retail organization, for example, may have a strategic culture that is fundamentally different from that of a manufacturing company or a technology leader. We have not found a definitive answer, but such speculation is certainly thought provoking. You may want to consider whether the specific macro-sector or industry in which you operate is subject to external forces and norms that shape its culture.

Look to your leader's style. The business press enjoys writing about the culture of General Electric, much of which was embodied in the vibrant personality of its former CEO, "Neutron Jack" Welch. In the years Welch served, the stories and legends that described him—in terms of management style, energy, ways of communicating, meetings, relationships with strategic partners and shareholders—constituted a set of cultural expectations that reflected not just the man but the culture he fostered to help implement his vision.

CREATING AND SUSTAINING STRATEGIC PERFORMANCE

Culture is shorthand for how an organization thinks and behaves, and no element of it is more important than the way the organization manages human performance. The question here is: To what extent is the strategy and its supporting culture embedded in the way an organization directs, manages, and rewards it people? The best organizations create and maintain a systematic discipline for managing human performance at every level to ensure strategic alignment.

In an organizational context, human performance comprises *a series of behaviors directed toward achievement of a specific goal.* Managing these behaviors is often seen as a simple matter of managing the responsible individuals or groups. Yet at every level employees will argue that their failure to behave in a certain way "isn't their fault"—often justifiably so.

One proven construct for understanding organizational behavior is the performance system model.[2] It describes certain key variables and their interaction—performance goals and the work environment, the employee, the behavior ("performance") itself, the consequences for behaving in a certain way, and the information or feedback provided about performance.

Aligning the Performance System

This crucial task is illustrated by the story of BHP's Long Products Division, a half-billion-dollar subsidiary of Australia's largest company. George Edgar assumed the leadership role when the division's survival was on the line. Once its future vision was clear, Edgar made sure that the implementation plan included a major project to redefine the workplace and in the process to ensure that the overall working environment and employee behavior were in complete alignment with the vision. He wanted to utilize the brainpower of individuals—to change their mindset and hence their behavioral responses to their role in implementing the division's strategic goals.

Edgar saw to it that all employees had the information and skills they needed to do their jobs and that they all understood the triggers provided for them to take action. These included clear objectives related to the strategic elements of their jobs. Priorities for each individual were also agreed upon.

Many of the best organizations go only this far to align the performance system with strategy. But Edgar knew better. Positive reinforcement for the achievement of objectives was accompanied by coaching, counseling, and when necessary, negative consequences for individuals who ignored the strategic dimension of their jobs.

As Edgar realized, such a performance system relies heavily on timely, accurate feedback to every employee in both formal and informal venues.

In summary, aligning strategy and performance requires a chief executive to:

- Explain why the organization and its employees must change
- Identify who is responsible for specific tasks and ensure that he or she has the requisite skills, information, and resources
- Communicate exactly what changes are needed in order to foster strategy implementation
- Provide clarity on the consequences and rewards for behaviors that support the strategy, and make sure these are followed through
- Provide the information and feedback on both corporate and individual performance against the organization's strategic objectives

A more technical description of this model is beyond the scope of this book; however, we encourage every executive to consider the potential impact on strategy implementation of the performance system approach to managing behavior.

Aligning the Culture

Getting an organization to modify or change its culture is not brain surgery. It's a lot tougher. But leaders must rise to the occasion, especially when there is a significant shift in strategy. Discipline is vital. Time and effort are required to identify and define the projects essential to strategic and cultural alignment. Though the nature of the projects around the softer elements of culture may differ from projects related to market entry and product development, the process does not. The result is the definition of a category of culture and performance projects in the Strategic Master Project Plan. We suggest this approach:

- Examine the existing culture and performance system through an analysis of behaviors and organizational artifacts to establish how well they serve the strategy and its implementation.
- Identify the gaps that need to be filled and the weaknesses that must be corrected.
- Design the projects that will bring systems, processes, behaviors, and attitudes into alignment with the strategy.
- Implement these projects within the framework of the Strategic Master Project Plan.
- Ensure that processes for reinforcing, promoting, and embedding the strategic culture are in place.

THE CEO'S INFLUENCE ON STRATEGIC CULTURE

While it takes an entire organization to set and implement strategy, there is no single person whose influence on a company's strategic culture and performance management systems is greater than that of the CEO. There are specific, tangible actions that the CEO can take to articulate, create, and sustain a strategically aligned culture. Here are several key imperatives:

- Take personal responsibility for walk-the-talk leadership on every facet of the culture. Model exemplary adherence to the basic beliefs. Stimulate, challenge, and support the top team in exercising ever more fruitful strategic thinking. Be the first to notice when a tempting short-term fix is off the strategy and should be avoided. Encourage a focus on the future in every meeting, and dodge the short-term pull of operational concerns. In short, strive to embody the attributes of culture that will help the strategy thrive and produce financial results.

- Work with the top team to ensure that the process of defining strategically aligned objectives for culture and performance management is as disciplined as every other aspect of implementing the strategy.
- Obtain the ownership and commitment of every employee to basic beliefs and other visible aspects of the cultural mix. Be prepared to debate, listen, and modify the content of your message as you involve employees in the quest for understanding prior to implementation.
- Decide how to use the organization's cultural heritage to support its strategic vision. If you have risen through the organization, you are in a unique position to understand which elements of the current culture are likely to support implementation, and which may harm it. If you have been brought in from outside, you will need to spend considerable time and effort gaining this insight.
- Promote action affecting every component of the performance system. Champion the development of people in accordance with strategically aligned expectations. Communicate the organization's intent continuously, so that strategically aligned behaviors are clearly defined. Make a firm commitment to seeing that the organization's reward systems foster desired behaviors, and ensure that the consequences are in balance throughout the organization.

AT TOWNGAS: CULTURE FOR THE FUTURE

The power of top management to effect successful strategy implementation through leadership and role-modeling has been admirably exploited by Alfred Chan's team at Towngas.

As we mentioned earlier, Chan himself modeled a wholehearted commitment to being close to the customer before a strategy formulation was ever undertaken. Since beginning strategy implementation several years ago, Chan relies on a systematic approach to fostering the culture required by the Towngas strategy.

When Chan's top team established the Towngas basic beliefs, it examined the specific outcomes it wanted to achieve with each stakeholder group. With employees, the team sought to promote an open-minded environment and encourage the expression of innovative ideas. Since the Towngas competitive advantage lay in its special relationship with customers, the greatest return on investment would come from bringing even better service—and a broader array of services—into existing markets. The key capability to be nurtured was this capacity for creativity, open-mindedness, innovation, and competence.

Early on, the team established opportunities for individual departments to initiate projects to improve quality and the return on investments. Chan especially wanted to encourage a mindset of responsibility at the front-line levels. Technicians, phone operators, and salespeople submitted their recommended approach on potential projects for judging by the executive committee of the company. The projects deemed most potentially fruitful were implemented under the direction of the top team.

After several years of encouraging this simple effort and many others, the Towngas culture has shifted significantly—so much, in fact, that a core team of 30 employees has now demonstrated the depth of innovative thinking that will be required for one difficult task—the development of Towngas activity in the massive China market.

Leadership has also been a central pillar of Towngas's strategy implementation. Based on the strategic vision, the executive committee identified 25 specific efforts that would fill gaps in their ability to achieve the top rung in customer service. Each of these Key Management Focuses (KMFs) is assigned to one of some 25 senior executives; he or she is responsible for translating the gap into a project that is monitored by the top team. Examples of these KMFs include improving communication between front-line and management levels, improving penetration of automatic meter reading, and establishing a unified purchasing policy to support expansion into China.

Both creativity and results are prized as measures of KMF achievements. As Chan says, "You have a group of senior executives and department managers, each holding a particular initiative. It may be directly related to a given department, or it may require action across the entire company. The leader must coordinate the project, identify the right partners and team members in other departments, and draw on their expertise to implement solutions."

Chan's approach is no simple lip-service nod to creativity. The ability of executives to model strategic behavior and obtain strategic results is built into the recognition and rewards of their own performance system. The top team demonstrates its own commitment by reviewing KMF progress in scheduled, biannual reviews. Chan says:

> **Sometimes, I walk into a company's waiting area and see some statement of their vision hanging on the wall, like "We want to be the best customer service company in southeast Asia." In China now, these are all very well written—very well dreamt!—but the problem is how to turn those dreams into action.**
>
> **A company must know how to motivate its people, how to give people the skills to implement strategic actions, how to follow up on their behaviors—in short, how to translate strategy into action. A strategically aligned culture and performance system are paramount.**

The top team also must maintain a relentless focus on perpetuating strategic thinking in every nook and cranny of the organization. Its own response—to the conflicting and complex demands of strategy and operations, the company's heritage and its future, and to disconnects that no longer serve the organization's purpose—will set the example.

To achieve success in strategy implementation, every organization must also build a systematic approach to communication so that expectations are clear. This is the subject of our next chapter.

CHAPTER

11

Implementation: Communicating Strategy

The most difficult thing about the implementation of a strategy is how you communicate it down to the working level within the organization. Too often, the people who are actually doing the work think, "Strategy doesn't mean anything to me, so I'll just ignore it and keep doing my thing the way I'm doing it."

But the people down on the floor are going to implement the strategy; therefore, they have to understand it. You have to keep communicating it to them, making the strategy relevant to business units, building it into how you operate, and then remind them that they—not the president or the CEO—are going to implement this strategy. Let them know how they're doing, how the company is doing, where it is strong, where it is weak. Communication is about making strategy a living process that the workforce can relate to.

—Jay F. Honeycutt, President
Lockheed Martin's Space Operations

At Xerox in the early 1970s, a bizarre event epitomized what was then the tradition of strategic secrecy. A board member received a phone call at international headquarters in London in which he was offered the opportunity to purchase access to a primary competitor's "long-range plan." He refused the offer in accord with Xerox's values at that time. The guilty party was eventually tracked down and convicted.

Typically, in those days, a company's strategy was sealed hermetically in the desk drawer of the CEO and shared with only a few trusted lieutenants. Disclosing even the most general intent of a strategy to all employees much less to the general public was seen as a huge threat to the organization's competitive edge.

Contrast that top-secret view with the advertisement placed by General Electric in the *Wall Street Journal*, reproduced here as Figure 11-1. With the text of this ad, GE makes its core strategic intentions explicit: "#1 in X business," "diversified financial services businesses and leading consumer businesses," "meet our commitments to inves-

---

WAS

Born over 100 years ago as a company of great ideas
and the people who have them.

IS

Leading global businesses: #1 in Medical Equipment.
#1 in Aircraft Engines. #1 in Engineered Thermoplastics.
#1 in Network Television. #1 in Power Generation Equipment.
#1 in Locomotives. #1 in Equipment Leasing.
A set of leading diversified financial services businesses and leading
consumer businesses. Triple A rating for 21 straight years . . .
Through good and bad economic cycles, we meet our commitments
to investors based on the strength of the GE business model.

WILL BE

As steadfastly committed to great growth ideas,
and the people who have them, as we have always been.
And poised to deliver results as we've always done. It's what we do.
GE: We bring good things to life.

Figure 11-1   Communicating Strategy—General Electric (Advertisement in the *Wall Street Journal*, April 17, 2002, sec. A.)

tors," "great growth ideas," "poised to deliver results." A classic conglomerate, GE has a Return/Profit Driving Force, and it goes on record here about its competitive advantage and the key capabilities ("strength of the GE business model," "ideas and the people who have them," a "Triple A rating") that support it.

GE's ad typifies a kind of positioning that was rare in the 1970s. Nowadays, nearly every organization, certainly every publicly held one, knows that much of its strategic vision will find its way into the public domain. In fact, most make plans to publicize these messages. The benefits of such communication now far outweigh any possible advantage a competitor might gain. It could even be argued that intentionally telling competitors about the strategy can serve as a pre-emptive strike, warning them to "keep off our patch." What's more, the loyalty and perceptions of customers and business partners undoubtedly will be strengthened through successfully communicating a well-conceived strategy.

On the internal front, there is simply no excuse for any enterprise to not communicate its strategy throughout the ranks. Failure to do so is a death sentence for strategy implementation. Like every other component of implementation, the process of communication is both an art and a rigorous discipline.

WHY COMMUNICATE?

In the previous chapter, we discussed the unity that a coherent culture and performance system brings. The same must be said of communication: It is a key strategic unifier.

The most cohesive support for implementation will be gained when the many internal and external stakeholders—for example, employees, trade unions, customers, banks, business partners, and shareholders— have the opportunity to understand, question, and embrace the strategic vision. Each of these audiences will certainly bring along some "baggage" as it is invited into the strategy forum. Employees may be feeling rather insecure since they know that a company's examination of strategy could mean change (or even trouble). Outside analysts and bankers may bring a healthy dose of skepticism, especially if there have been failed attempts at implementing strategy in the past. Trade unions and their members may be outright suspicious, anticipating a new deal that might disrupt their agenda.

Such concerns are not unfounded. The news will not necessarily be positive, or easy, for every group or individual. Some employees may be asked to take on new assignments; others may lose their jobs. Suppliers may be expected to meet more restrictive standards and tighter schedules. Investors may be asked to accept lower short-term financial returns or a dilution of their shareholding to fund strategic investments. Nonetheless, every stakeholder ultimately recognizes and respects a strategy that shows clear purpose and direction. The only way to convey such an intent is to communicate it. Most of those affected will find that they have an important role in the organization's future success.

Why communicate? First, to promote ownership throughout the organization and by external audiences. Stakeholders must be persuaded of the rigor of the process undertaken, the validity of the conclusions reached, and the attendant opportunities. Only with this firm sense of ownership will the backbone of a corporate culture support strategy implementation.

A second reason is equally important. When stakeholders understand the strategy, they are an important source of feedback. Given the opportunity, internal audiences offer a view from the trenches that helps put strategic givens into context and provides a valuable reality check on their feasibility. Shareholders, investors, customers, and suppliers may also have insights that will strengthen implementation and identify any gaps.

Communicating strategy is also a critical piece of the performance system puzzle. Most powerful is the translation of the big-picture vision into the specific expectations for performance by individuals and groups. Armed with information that speaks directly to the actions and behaviors that support strategy, employees are able to understand the impact of their own contributions. Top managers should be prepared to examine the overall corporate performance system as well, taking the lead to demonstrate that the need for balance between strategic and operational objectives will be resolved.

However, information is not enough. Employees must also be motivated and committed to change. Every strategic player, internally and externally, should understand "what does this mean for me?" When communication is handled appropriately, it helps every employee develop the motivation needed to align his or her own actions and priorities with the strategy.

Finally—and this is the ultimate goal—communication must lead to behavior change. This is no one-time event. At every opportunity, communication about the specific changes individuals and teams are asked to accept help them make the leap to action. Strategy should inform the processes of setting goals, developing job descriptions and performance expectations, evaluating priorities, managing projects, acquiring new skills, implementing systems and processes, and modeling new values and beliefs. These events signal that "the times they are a-changing," and are a call to climb on board.

THE TOP TEAM: GUIDING COMMUNICATION

The strategy formulation and strategy implementation teams bear responsibility for helping to craft the communication plan and overseeing its execution.

Typically, a top team chooses to consult with internal and/or external professionals in communications and public relations. The first task is to explain to these experts the process used to set strategy and the content of the strategic profile and the Strategic Master Project Plan. They can then facilitate the entire communication effort with a deep understanding of the company's strategic goals and of any requirements for confidentiality.

The Who and What of the Communication Plan

To determine the nature of any communication plan, the team must consider the nature of each audience, as well as the content and format of the message. The top team must define which messages (the what) will be communicated to which audiences (the who).

Who needs to know about strategy? The list of stakeholders varies from organization to organization, but the answers to these questions point the way: "Whom do we need to help us achieve our strategic vision?" "To what degree do we expect the members of this audience to affect implementation, given that they understand the strategy and their role in completing certain tasks?"

Criteria should be developed to determine the messages for each constituency. Not everything is communicated to everyone. A message about the firm's thrust for growth and business, for example, will be delivered with a different emphasis and level of detail depending on the audience; middle managers, plant workers, and investment bankers need to understand different aspects of the overall message. Messages are to be crafted and "packaged" in a unique way for each constituent—a job for the professionals.

Certain aspects of the strategy must almost certainly be communicated across the entire organization. Central messages are drawn directly from the strategic vision and the Strategic Master Project Plan. The basic beliefs, for example, must be shared with every single employee in the organization and some key external stakeholders. Yet only certain employees will need to know the specifics of return and growth expectations.

To identify what each constituency needs to know, consider these types of questions:

- Do members of this group work in an area critically affected by the new strategy?
- What is the extent and nature of the changes this group will be asked to make?
- Will this audience be key in the development of new capabilities?
- Will this group provide key resources for implementation?
- Is buy-in from this group essential to successful implementation?
- What will happen if this group is not pulling with us?

The result of this work is a strategy communication matrix; an example of the first cut of this work, showing only primary messages and major stakeholder groups, is shown in Figure 11-2.

The top team must ensure that all critical messages have been identified, as well as all key audiences. The privately held U.S. firm mentioned earlier and owned by more than 30 family members had simply paid annual dividends and never told its owners anything about the company's strategy or performance for years—until we worked with them when the company began to underperform. It deeply regretted this oversight (or was it arrogance?), as there was no committed support for the top team. The pitfalls of overlooking components of the who and what are many, and potentially serious.

Key
- ✓ Need to know
- ? May need to know, revisit criteria
- ▢ No current need to know

Stakeholders		Elements of the Strategic Profile and Master Plan							
		Strategy Process Adopted	Basic Beliefs	Vision Statement	Basis of Competitive Advantage	Product/Market Matrix	Key Capability Requirements	Growth and Return Expectations	Strategic Master Project Plan
Internal	Board	✓	✓	✓	✓	✓	✓	✓	✓
	Managers	✓	✓	✓	✓	✓	✓	✓	✓
	Employees	✓	✓	✓	✓	Sales force only	✓		✓
External	Trade Unions	✓	✓	✓	✓		✓	?	
	Key Investors	✓		✓	✓			✓	
	Analysts	✓		✓	✓			✓	
	Bankers	✓		✓	✓			✓	
	Customers	✓	✓	✓	✓				
	Suppliers	✓	✓	✓	✓	?			
	Advertising, PR, & Marketing Advisers	✓	✓	✓	✓	✓	✓	✓	?
	Joint Venture or Alliance Partners	✓	✓	✓	✓	✓	✓	✓	✓

Figure 11-2 A Sample Communication Matrix: Who and What

The Components of the Communication Plan

Based on the communication matrix, a project plan is developed and integrated into the overall Strategic Master Project Plan. Analyzing and planning for potential problems, understanding and applying what has been learned in each phase of the project, and executing the plan with discipline are no less important here than in critical product and market efforts. Each cell in the matrix represents a subproject to be designed and implemented. The plan must address the following components:

The Strategic Message

The initial purpose of communication is to simply convey information about the strategy and the process used to formulate it. The format should be user friendly and tailored to each audience with the simple intent of complementing the message's content.

A Means of Testing the Listener's Understanding of the Strategic Message

Feedback about the message must be captured and incorporated into subsequent communications. Telling is not enough. A typical format, such as a PowerPoint presentation followed by a brief question-and-answer period, will certainly not meet the needs of those whose work directly affects strategic success. A strategic vision and how it will be implemented entails complex, subtle concepts; nuance is important, and many opportunities must be created for testing understanding, receiving and giving feedback, and simply discussing the strategic messages.

An Understanding of the Costs

Creating the various messages and providing for their distribution to audiences is only part of the story. Top teams must also accept that the time of every person involved in both presenting the message and receiving it is time missed from other responsibilities—but well worth the investment.

A Schedule for Releasing Information and Obtaining Feedback

Plan for the appropriate sequence of messages for specific audiences, and include prompt followup to reinforce the communication.

Evidence of Top Management's Direct Involvement

Ensure that the company's top management takes responsibility for delivering strategic communications. Advisers may be asked to articulate and package strategic communication, but their role ends there. Whenever possible, the CEO and members of the strategy formulation team should take command of the communication process, and be available for give-and-take discussion.

Built-In Feedback Mechanisms

Build in mechanisms for gathering feedback on the strategy and its implementation. The company's leaders must assume responsibility for receiving this feedback and acting on it as part of their systematic review of implementation.

Every communication plan must provide the opportunity for feedback. Inevitably, there will be questions about the strategy itself and its implementation. Rather than avoid what could be controversial areas, top teams should see healthy debate as an opportunity to improve strategic literacy and forge commitment. Feedback from stakeholders is one of the most fruitful sources for monitoring and updating strategy. Communication is not a discrete task that ends on a given date; instead, it contributes to the ongoing assessment of the vision. We'll look more closely at this process in our next chapter.

Inevitably, conflicting points of view will emerge as the strategy and its implications are shared. Again, the top team is responsible for seeing that channels are available to gather these views, and that they are provided in an appropriate manner and time frame. Even when strategic news is unsettling or very negative for those adversely affected, communication must be honest and direct. This is not a situation in which no news is good news—and employees know it.

The Timing of Communication

When to begin? Although communication is a key part of strategy implementation, there is good reason to begin preliminary efforts much earlier, even before strategy formulation begins. The corporate rumor mill is not to be underestimated, and there will be plenty of creative talk about the strategy exercise the top team is about to undertake.

An early communication plan will go far to quiet rumors and reassure employees. A CEO should consider these questions: Who should be told about the forthcoming project, the process to be used, and the involvement of others outside the top team? How much information should be shared? When is the right time to go "public" internally? Who will be responsible for this communication, and how will it be accomplished? "Early and often" is almost never the wrong answer when it comes to communicating.

THE GOLDEN RULES OF COMMUNICATION

Throughout the process of communicating strategy, the top team should be mindful of these golden rules:

- The top team carries the brunt of the responsibility. The involvement of the CEO and/or members of the original strategy formulation team is a powerful message in and of itself, and they should be a part of as many communication channels as conceivable.
- Stick together. No matter what the ups and downs of the strategy process have been, the top team must present an absolutely united front. The slightest chink in the armor or rumbling in the corridor invalidates the entire communication effort.
- Face-to-face communication is always better. We are reminded of the hapless CEO who simply sent out ineffective videos. On a topic as crucial as strategy, doubt and controversy are givens. When communication takes place on a personal level, any potentially misleading messages can be clarified on the spot.
- Involve the supervisor or manager closest to the targeted individuals or groups. In order to answer critical questions about how specific actions and behaviors will change, the person who will be responsible for monitoring those changes must be on hand, alongside the CEO or top team member.
- Know when to listen. Every communication effort provides an opportunity for dialogue. The potential lessons to be learned are too valuable to overlook.
- Skip the dazzle and focus on the message. Occasionally, the purpose of communicating strategy is lost in the attempt to package the message appealingly. Don't underestimate any of your stakeholders—they know the difference between fluff and stuff.

- Engage your audience. There's an art to motivating people, and communication must be persuasive if it is to influence each individual to change on-the-job behavior.
- Connect every message with an action to be taken or a plan to be implemented. If your constituents are expected to make changes, they need to understand how to do that and what the next steps are.

And if those are the golden rules, this final rule is etched in platinum:

- No communication is successful unless it answers the question "What does this mean for me?" This is the core message for every stakeholder. When you're asking individuals and groups to change their behavior and align their efforts with the strategic vision, they'd better understand what you want them to do—and why.

This platinum rule is well understood at Towngas. There, an inner circle of roughly 50 employees makes up the Strategy Ambassador Club. This group receives the first reports whenever strategy is updated. Four or five times a year, Managing Director Chan addresses the group to explain key aspects of the strategy and how front-line employees should respond to align their own roles. Chan gives examples to help employees understand every connection: how strategy relates to individual jobs, to departmental expectations, to traditions, to every aspect of the Towngas culture. The ambassadors then talk with individuals and small groups in debriefing sessions with front-line workers.

The top team supports the Club so strongly that membership in it is a reward for top employees. Six employees are nominated to the Ambassador Club each year; they are role models for their peers, and they are directly exposed to the strategic thinking of Chan and other senior executives.

GETTING IT RIGHT

Several of our clients have taken on the communication challenge under circumstances of tremendous change. Here are three who got it right.

The Bristol and West Bank

As mentioned earlier, the Bristol and West Bank lost its way after a period of roller-coaster diversification in the 1980s. When the dust had settled, the bank found itself near the bottom of industry ratings amid much speculation about mergers and acquisitions, restructuring, and a generally turbulent period in the financial world.

Under new CEO John Burke, Bristol and West adopted a strategy in 1994 that was focused on its core business activities—mortgages, savings, and investments. Among the constituents for its communications were employees, financial institutions, and millions of customers. Burke and his top team embarked immediately on a series of programs to communicate with and train middle managers and executives to ensure that they understood the new strategy and their role in it. Further, the team also ensured that the middle-management audience was prepared to cascade the strategic message through the entire firm, in every branch nationwide.

Immediately following this effort, the company undertook a series of 47 presentations to London's financial community, explaining its change in strategic direction and return to its core business. These presentations were exceptionally well received by an audience that had all but written off the Bristol and West as it struggled under the financial stresses of the hard-nosed 1990s.

Finally, the firm undertook a major advertising campaign built primarily around powerful television commercials. These were aimed at current and future customers, and they reinforced the message that the Bristol and West had returned to its roots—to what mattered most and what it did best. This scope and clarity of communication about the strategy differentiated the firm from its competitors, and it began to succeed.

During the strategy process, the top team had one overriding question: Once we have set our strategy correctly, can we do it alone, or should we find one or more partners? After some flirtation with potential suitors, the Bank of Ireland made a bid for the company. This overture was accepted, and the match has since proven to have been made in heaven, for both parties. In fact, Denis Hanrahan, then head of Group Corporate Development for the Bank of Ireland, has made it clear that key factors in the bank's decision to acquire Bristol and West were these: the clarity of its strategy; the commitment and solidarity of top executives Burke, Jeff Warren (now CEO), Ian Kennedy, and Kevin Flanagan; and the sense that the organization was united behind a common purpose.

The Savoy Group of Hotels

The Savoy Group, now owned by the U.S. real estate investment corporation Blackstone, was in trouble when Ramon Pajares was appointed CEO. As his team began to formulate strategy, Pajares knew that effective communication would be pivotal to successful implementation. The company had been privately held for many years, run as a personal fiefdom by the head of a very traditional family, and was taken over by Trust House Forte, which had appointed Pajares. Since the hotel industry has a very large proportion of employees who are on the front line, dealing directly with customers, Pajares' insight was not rocket science—though it might have been to the previous owners!

Once the strategy had been set, Pajares decided that the first step in his communication plan would be to mail letters addressed to all 2000 employees at home, explaining how they would be involved in shaping the future of the company. For his next step, he looked no further than his own front door, inviting every single employee to a series of presentations in the Savoy Theatre that is an integral part of the world-famous Savoy Hotel. Over a period of several weeks, Pajares and his top team personally conducted these communication sessions, which outlined the group's strategy and each employee's role in the plan to restore the Savoy as the world's premier hotel group. Later, managers followed up on the message with detailed information for every individual.

As we noted earlier, the group outperformed its goals 2 years ahead of plan. Pride and profitability returned.

British Airways Engineering and Maintenance Division

Some years ago we worked with the late Alistair Cumming, head of British Airways Engineering and Maintenance Division, to facilitate a functional strategy. The outcome was mind-bending for British Airways: The new strategy called for restructuring his division as a separate business unit. As Robert Heller, founding editor of *Management Today* and widely published author, described in the business press when the strategy was made public, "Taking a cost center and turning it into a successful business is never easy. The new strategy was to deliver the optimum use of planes to BA, reducing the costs associated with flying hours and landing costs."[1] And as the ultimate in business unit mentality, the division was expected to make a profit!

For British Airways, this required an extraordinary change in culture. New work practices, new beliefs and values, effective cost management, head count reductions—these were some of the mantras that required the collaboration of thousands of employees represented by a dozen (not always collaborative) trade unions.

Cumming understood immediately that a world-class communication effort would be needed to build strategic coherence and consistency throughout the organization. He put tremendous effort into close collaboration between management, employees, and trade union representatives to communicate the organization's focus immediately and repeatedly.

In just 2 years, a remarkably short period, the division's turnaround had been implemented. Cumming said at the time, "When difficulties arise, you must not let them get in the way of strategy—if you do, you are lost." He believed passionately in the power of focus, leading from the front, and the imperative to communicate, communicate, communicate!

THE COMMUNICATIONS PAYOFF

In the immortal words of the late President Lyndon Johnson, "I'd rather have them inside the tent pissing out than outside the tent pissing in." In order to involve its stakeholders fully, a world-class firm makes sure they are fully informed. It's a discipline that pays handsome dividends.

Every top team must also remember the power of implicit, as well as formally planned, communication. The resolution of a product or market issue, the language used in meetings to review implementation plans—these and many other leadership behaviors are also a part of the message. External stakeholders will certainly watch for congruency between the official communication effort and the implicit "body language" of the organization as it takes the next steps. Leaders, like the rest of us, are always judged more by their actions than by their words.

When every member of a play's cast and crew is reading from the same script, its progress toward world-class performance is rapid. Once the cast learns its lines, the rate of progress jumps dramatically. Communicating strategy provides the unity of a common script across the organization and beyond, so that all constituencies can play their roles more effectively.

When communication is built into the Strategic Master Project Plan, and especially into the ongoing monitoring of strategy, it offers the top team an opportunity to improve their work through incorporating the front-line view. A disciplined communication effort provides as many opportunities for the top team to learn as to instruct.

Most essentially, communication drives behavior changes in the corporate culture and individual performance that make implementation possible. When every player is informed, listened to, motivated, and committed to the effort, there are no excuses.

CHAPTER

12

Keeping It Evergreen: Strategy Renewal

One of the greatest failures ever to anticipate a competitive threat happened not just to a single company, or even a single industry, but to the entire Western industrial complex.

In the early 1970s, not only huge corporations but also entire industries failed to foresee the competitive attack that was brewing across the Pacific among their Japanese competitors. The threat that loomed was startling in both its scope and speed as it picked up steam over the next decade. Western electronic consumer goods like cameras and televisions were toppled from their pedestals on the basis of Japanese quality and pricing. The automobile and motorcycle industries succumbed quickly to a similar onslaught. Even the Western steel industry felt the effects.

At Xerox during much of this period, management in Southeast Asia tried—and failed despite its best efforts—to persuade top management in the United States of the threat posed by inexpensive, reliable desktop copiers. To this day, Xerox has not fully recovered.

In short, Western manufacturers were felled by a treacherous case of strategic myopia.

The failings of Western industry at this critical juncture in the evolution of the global marketplace were those that continue to confront organizations today. Its players failed to monitor indicators that were both observable and measurable; to review the implications of the obvious shifts; and to update their own strategic visions to meet the challenge head on.

The fifth and final phase of the strategy process challenges the top team to ask these questions: Given our strategic vision and plan for implementation, what could go differently from what we've anticipated, and why? How will we know if it occurs? And what will we do when it does? Answering these questions ensures that the strategy will be "evergreen."

It takes process and discipline to monitor the health of the strategy. Vital signs must be recorded, presenting symptoms challenged, and the true causes found. The treatment plan needs to be informed by feedback on the patient's progress. Recovery must be monitored, and any external threats that would compromise healing must be minimized.

Although an evergreen strategy process requires the skills of others to identify and analyze data, the top team remains responsible for nurturing the strategy and for calling the shots when change is required. Its ability to continually renew strategy is the ultimate test of leadership.

MONITORING THE STRATEGY

There are only two basic questions about the success of any undertaking: As the old adage goes, "Are we doing the right things, and are we doing things right?" In the strategy process, the top team closes the loop by constantly monitoring both the continuing viability of the strategy and its implementation—in other words, is our strategy succeeding?

Jay Honeycutt of Lockheed Martin says that slipups in this phase can make or break the entire strategy process:

> **You'd better be serious about strategy because it requires a continuous commitment not only of yourself but of your first-line management. And it's not going to happen overnight; you'd better be willing to persevere. You should be flexible enough to adapt to changes in the marketplace if they occur. The worst thing you could do is have a rigorously defined strategy that spawns a train going so fast that you can't get it to change direc-**

**tion if the market falls hard underneath you. You must continu-
ally revisit the strategy, making sure that it remains consistent
with the marketplace.**

Answering the following four questions—two on implementation,
two on viability—will help you understand and define the territory you
need to monitor.

*1. How well are we implementing the projects in our Strategic Master Proj-
ect Plan?* In the chapter on creating the Strategic Master Project Plan,
we noted that an important component is the ongoing monitoring of
each project. The strategy implementation team will be the central
clearinghouse for this information. With the assistance of a project support office and the project teams themselves, the implementation team
will monitor the progress of every project, subproject, and individual
task against these criteria:

- Is the project meeting its objectives, at the required level of
  quality?
- How does our progress measure up against the expected time-
  lines established?
- Are we staying within the expected budget of human and financial resources?
- Has anything changed to cause us to revisit the priority of
  projects?

The top team's involvement in reviewing project progress will vary
with the nature of the organization and the complexity of the plan.
Some companies may review only those projects for which the deviations are very significant or whose failure could irreversibly derail the
strategy. Others may focus on a limited set of criteria, such as those
above, or conduct a regular monthly overview.

In any case, the top team's commitment must be clear—including
its own adherence to the project management discipline adopted and
the process for assessing the priority of potential new projects.

As we noted earlier, 25 senior executives at Towngas are asked to take
extraordinary responsibility for the management of critical implementa-

tion projects, or Key Management Focuses. The top team's review of these projects is scheduled at monthly intervals, with each project coming before the team twice a year. Alfred Chan explains this approach:

> **The top team has to generate a habit through which progress on these projects will be reported in a systematic way. Reports are not enough; we ask for presentations in person, so that there can be two-way communication. And we involve the entire senior team, not just the chief executive, because its members represent every aspect of the business and can contribute their expertise to these key actions.**

Some enterprises integrate the preparation of annual operating plans into a project-oriented net of templates that help identify and plan major activities. Annual plans are then simply the financial roll-up of the various projects that will be executed. At Hallmark International, this approach has subsumed their traditional planning methodology, saving time, money, and frustration and ensuring that plans are focused on the vital few activities required for strategic success.

2. Is strategy driving the decisions made in our organization? Progress on the Strategic Master Project Plan is only one measure of implementation success. Just as important is how effectively new behaviors have been implemented to support strategy and align the efforts of the organization.

The most critical elements in this shift are those already discussed: clear and meaningful communication, the alignment of corporate culture and performance management with the strategy, and a supportive infrastructure.

One could argue that it is the sum of every decision made that determines whether strategy implementation has been successful. The quality of decision making is felt in every activity: product development, marketing and sales, human capability development, hiring and promotions, operational improvements, capital expenditures, and information management.

The top team plays a vital role in both modeling and monitoring the strategic alignment of decisions. It must be on the lookout for managerial "lone rangers" who operate as though immune from strategic imperatives, posing real threats to both implementation and strategic success. Senior managers should be asked these two central questions at every opportunity:

- How are your decisions consistent with the strategy?
- How are you institutionalizing strategy in your area of responsibility to ensure coherence and consistency?

When the Bristol and West Bank returned to its roots, it instituted a system to track decisions made at every level, right down to those made during interactions with customers in its network of hundreds of branches. The nature of these decisions was analyzed and measured against the strategic profile. When outdated decision-making criteria from the previous strategy were being used, executives took action to correct the cause and bring decision making in line.

Examples of decisions that are hot-wired to an organization's strategic intent include:

- Are we allocating our resources to those product/market combinations with the highest emphasis?
- Are we building our key capabilities through the appropriate mix of recruitment, training, and development?
- Does our marketing mix, particularly our advertising and promotional intent, reflect our strategic intent?

One potential concern: If the strategy itself is flawed—that is, if it no longer reflects the realities among suppliers and customers or it is not specific enough to guide action—then managers and their employees may face an impossible task. Executives may be forced to deliberately weigh market realities against the strategic intent—a tough situation at best!

3. Are the environmental assumptions we made during strategy formulation still valid? The assumptions made about internal and external environments during the initial phase of strategic intelligence gathering are the bedrock on which every other component of the strategy rests. If an environmental tremor—or an earthquake—shakes those assumptions, the strategy may well be in trouble.

For example, the rapidity of the dot.com bust, the rapid growth in Internet usage, the opening of China for trade, the remarkable technological leapfrogging of a competitor—these and many other sea changes in the global environment have forced the world's best strategic thinkers to think again.

One pre-emptive tactic: When assumptions about the economy, governmental policy, market size, competitors, and the like are first articulated, they should be recorded in quantitative terms whenever possible. For example, it is much easier to spot and measure a deviation from a quantified projection—for example, "The number of potential customers (urban-dwelling, earning $35,000 plus) in Scotland will increase by 25 percent over the next 5 years"—than from a vaguer formulation.

Periodic evaluation of environmental assessments, based on measurable parameters, must be built into the ongoing strategy process. The top team again must insist on accurate, current reporting and shoulder the responsibility for its review.

The government-sponsored Industrial Development Agency of Ireland (IDA) offers an example of how strategy needs reformulation when there is a significant change in the environment. In many respects, Ireland was considered the poor cousin of Europe well into the 1980s. Its economy was one of the least developed, and it had a low rate of growth, relatively high unemployment, a weak infrastructure, and a workforce less skilled than that of its European competitors. In fact, Ireland was a major recipient of aid from the European Union to assist in its development.

Beginning in 1990, the IDA, under the leadership of CEO Kieran McGowan, began to play a significant role in its economic growth as well. The IDA spearheaded efforts to attract jobs and investment and encourage overseas companies to locate operations in the nation.

Over the next 8 to 9 years, the IDA attracted literally hundreds of firms to Ireland, many of them American and Japanese. Most of these firms took up residence in or near the city of Dublin. They were lured with financial subsidies from the Irish government and the European Union, tax breaks, and even specific infrastructure projects (to improve transport, housing, education, and health systems) that benefited employers as well as their Irish employees.

Against this environmental background and its charter to create wealth through attracting as many projects and jobs as possible, the IDA was highly successful. But the environmental conditions had begun to change. The IDA itself and its government sponsor had been monitoring them closely. They realized that, as a result of the shift, what had worked for the IDA in the past would also need to change. The IDA needed a new strategy.

By the late 1990s, Ireland's economy had seen a dramatic turnaround. It enjoyed full employment, low inflation, and a greatly improved infrastructure—in no small measure due to the success of the IDA. Yet this very success brought new concerns to the fore.

Early in the recovery period, the jobs created required relatively few skills. But during the 1990s, the IDA attracted more companies with greater skill and technology requirements. Despite the improvements in Irish schools and universities, too few workers had the IT, linguistic, and other specialized skills required. Ireland's success worked against it as well. As the economy strengthened and European Union policies evolved, the financial inducements offered to companies were not as easily granted. Ireland was forced to compete more on its own merits.

With the support of Denis Hanrahan, who was the IDA chairman at the time, McGowan's team set out to create a new strategic vision. It was forced to think the unthinkable, turning from a strategy of volume (in both projects attracted and jobs provided) to one of value added. Rather than welcoming companies in industries—textiles, for example—that needed cheap labor and only a modest skill base, the IDA would target industries whose potential jobs met a tough set of criteria, including information technology, pharmaceuticals, and finance. Ireland would need to recruit former Irish emigrants and new immigrants from other nations to fill both skilled and unskilled positions. The goods and services produced, tax revenues generated, and salaries paid would provide significantly greater return. The economic multiplier effect would also be greater.

Dublin was also suffering from mounting house prices as well as a housing shortage, and from the strain on its infrastructure due to its rapid growth in the previous years. The imbalance in investment between it and the rest of the country was huge. The IDA thus adopted a regional strategy to distribute economic gains more evenly, and it focused on several second-rank cities as future homes for incoming companies.

The team had to turn its back on what had been a winning formula and accept new norms in the external environment that were in part of its own making. The creative task was enormous—to formulate a strategy that would deliver better results but with less financial support for its customers. Yet the task was completed, and the Irish government accepted the IDA team's recommendations. Under Sean Dorgan, McGowan's successor, the IDA has reinvented itself, and it continues to fulfill its task as a major facilitator of wealth creation.

In another example, Jay Honeycutt relates these experiences at Lockheed Martin, also in the arena of shifting environmental assumptions:

> We set our strategy in the mid-1990s with the intent of taking our expertise and software to the commercial market, based on our experience as NASA contractors for more than 30 years. In 1997 and 1998, dot.com companies were going through the roof, software sales were escalating, and major systems integrators had more work than they could handle. The commercial sector seemed ripe for the transfer of skills from our NASA business to a potential new marketplace.
>
> We realigned certain aspects of our organizational structure to ensure that we were competitive on cost, and we entered the commercial market, quickly building a respectable customer base.
>
> Then the bottom fell out of dot.coms, of course, and the picture we had seen in 1998 rapidly disappeared—and our opportunities disappeared pretty much with them. So we have not been able to benefit from the commercial market to the degree that we had hoped. Now we are re-examining our strategy to decide whether to stick with a split in emphasis as was originally decided or to refocus on our fundamental government-sponsored business.

In a world where the rate of change is increasing exponentially, the team that stays focused on the continuing validity of strategic assumptions is well ahead of the game.

4. Is our strategy viable? Is it driving our success in the marketplace? Viability is both the purpose of strategy and its ultimate reality test. The top team must habitually revisit these questions, which are the toughest of all:

- Have we selected the best possible Driving Force?
- Has our relative emphasis on certain products and markets produced the expected results?
- Have the areas identified as priorities for growth and new business proven fruitful?
- Has our source of competitive advantage proven to be a significant one?
- Are we successfully developing or acquiring the key capabilities our strategy requires?
- Have our basic beliefs provided the underpinnings for both business practice and the culture needed to sustain the strategy?
- How are we performing against our financial expectations and other key indicators of strategic success?

The answers to the final question above may well be informed by creating a strategic balanced scorecard to consider a wide range of items. Key indicators of strategic success typically include these types of measures:

- *Financial expectations*: Operating profit, cash flow, return on net assets, revenue growth
- *Product and market performance:* Sales by product and market, shifts in product/market emphasis, rate of new-product introduction, penetration of new consumer or geographic markets, successful withdrawal from product and market segments
- *Competitive assessments:* Relative market share, product and market successes of competitors, significant actions by competitors
- *External assessments:* Feedback from shareholders, financial analysts, and the media; customer satisfaction ratings and other feedback
- *Internal assessments:* Employee feedback, performance measures for individuals and groups

RENEWING THE STRATEGY

Just as the top team reviews trends in order to unearth corporate implications during the strategic intelligence phase, it must review the answers to the questions above about ongoing strategic health, and ask: What are the implications for the strategy of any deviations identified? Are the deviations significant enough to require action?

Generally, a strategy must be reevaluated either when relatively small deviations occur on a regular basis or when there is a major deviation. The team must avoid two pitfalls, however. First, it must confirm that the deviation—say, a dropoff in financial return—is the direct result of the strategy rather than of flaws on the operational side. For example, a failure in the coherence of decision making may reflect inadequate communication of the strategy or inconsistent role modeling, rather than a strategic weakness. A project that is off track may simply require the leadership of a more experienced manager.

Second, the team must undertake its review without succumbing to blaming, posturing, and finger pointing. The strategy process is undertaken from the outset in the context of uncertainty, and external events inevitably influence its success. Just as the future cannot be known, the past cannot be changed, and the team must rally to its shared vision.

The team's response to a confirmed need for updating the strategy will vary according to the nature of the threat. A single failing—for example, a weakness in product development—may be so significant that the source of competitive advantage must be reviewed and resources reallocated to boost performance.

Similarly, an extremely compelling external event might force the team to reconsider the entire product/market matrix, or even the Driving Force itself. Think of the effect of the events of September 11 on financial services or security firms in the United States, for example. Such a full-scale review before the end of the strategic time frame will only be necessary in exceptional circumstances.

No matter how well things are going, the simple passage of time is reason enough for a thorough strategy review. The appropriate interval depends on the original strategic time frame and the overall pace of change in the industry. At a minimum, an annual review period of several days should be anticipated.

STICKING TO IT

Because they bear responsibility for the ongoing vitality of the strategy, senior executives should also audit their own priorities. What percentage of time is spent on facilitating strategy implementation? On the review of strategic indicators? On the continuing communication of strategy and building of a strategically aligned culture and performance system? And for each of these areas, what is the potential payoff?

Most CEOs and their teams are well aware of the potential vulnerabilities in their strategies. Any team that follows a disciplined process for formulating and implementing strategy has already wrestled with the tough questions that test its efficacy.

Some issues that arise will naturally come to the attention of top management whether or not they are identified through formal strategy monitoring. A prospective merger or an unusual opportunity for entering a lucrative market will not be overlooked; intuitively, these deserve, and will receive, immediate review.

The very best executives know that this final phase of strategy is of no less importance than the formulation and implementation phases. But too often, it receives the least attention. After the emotional peak of formulating a strategy and the complexity of planning implementation, few top teams are able to maintain their stamina. There may be two reasons for this. First, these activities clearly may be seen as a "grind"; they are never ending and require continuing commitment. But also, the rate of change in this new century makes an evergreen approach to strategy both difficult to achieve and too critically important to ignore.

At the same time, we do not advocate a constant cycle of monitoring, reviewing, and updating for its own sake. Monthly shifts in direction will convey a disturbing sense of inconsistency to the organization's stakeholders. There is a fine art in seeking the balance between responding to change and staying the course, and senior executives must use their judgment to find that equilibrium.

Three types of companies exemplify differing attitudes toward change. *Survivor companies* demonstrate an ability to *adapt* quickly to changes in their business environment if this is necessary to maintain strategic focus, relevance, and viability. The more quickly they can adapt, the more competitive they remain. *Successful companies* learn to *anticipate* change and alter their strategies in advance of such change, whether the impact will be negative or positive. These companies are always ahead of the game, and they are the envy of their less nimble competitors.

World-class companies dictate the nature and pace of change. The dominance of such remarkable firms is unbeatable; they define and redefine the very industries in which they participate, even drive the value chain, from suppliers to customers. Especially in this day and age of rapid change, the advantage is huge in being the one that is in charge.

The strategy of one consumer products company opens with the words: "We will *redefine* and *own* our category worldwide." That is as strong a statement of intent as can be expressed. The strategy goes on to describe how the company will achieve its goals by adapting to change, anticipating change, but—whenever possible—dictating change.

Any company would like to attain such a status. The rigor of strategy monitoring, reviewing, and updating is the secret weapon of such companies; they will be the standouts of the future.

In the next chapter, we will raise questions that challenge CEOs and their top teams to think beyond their current strategic time frame. The ultimate measure of today's strategy is its strength as a platform for the strategy that will eventually follow. While the five-phase strategy model is challenging in its own right, we invite you to consider what will happen next—to think beyond the current strategy and far into the future.

CHAPTER

13

Strategy in the Twenty-First Century

Today, not even the most casual observer could ignore the uncertainty pervading our planet. Airplanes fly into skyscrapers with calculated purpose. Hot new dot.coms disintegrate seemingly overnight. A U.S. presidential election is decided by nine Supreme Court justices. Nine European nations have adopted a single currency, and Japan continues on the edge of economic disaster. The Y2K crisis is long forgotten, the global stock market boom is bust, and the threat of devastating warfare looms again in the Middle East and South Asia. The cloning of humans is possible.

The corporate landscape is just as unpredictable. Half of the world's largest 50 economies are now corporations rather than nations. Unlikely alliances and unforeseeable failures have given the most level-headed of leaders reason to hesitate. Who could have predicted the current state of affairs at Daimler-Chrysler, HP-Compaq, AOL/Time Warner, Enron, Arthur Andersen, Marconi, Railtrack, or Vivendi, even just 2 or 3 years ago?

What of strategy in the midst of this turmoil? Is strategic thinking still relevant? Is it even possible to rely on a cohesive strategic construct in these times?

Let's look back to the beginning of this strategic journey. The starting point for every team is the assessment of the external environment in the political, socioeconomic, technological, and competitive arenas. What are the significant trends in these areas in these opening years of the new century?

We have been struck by three of the many startling trends that have emerged. First, the immediate devastation of the September 11 attacks has been followed by political and economic shockwaves whose effects will likely shape the next several years, if not decades. Technological developments have also transformed the way companies of every size and scale think about their means of influencing consumers, taking products to market, and forming alliances with suppliers. And on the horizon looms the not-so-silent Chinese giant—perhaps poised to dominate trade with the West for the first time in many centuries.

These are diverse yet representative examples of the magnitude of change leaders can (and sometimes cannot) anticipate. The next years will be more unpredictable than those of the last decade, perhaps wildly so. These examples underscore the importance of a sound, clear vision, coupled with the power and flexibility inherent in best-practice strategic process.

CHINA: THE EMERGING GIANT

Is China a threat or an opportunity? For most of us, the jury is still out and will be for some time. One thing is clear: This economic behemoth cannot be ignored.

In 2001, China experienced not only ongoing and impressive organic growth; it also attracted more foreign direct investment than South Korea, Thailand, Malaysia, Indonesia, Singapore, and Vietnam *combined*. Japan is still in the doldrums, unlikely to recover for many years, and the Asian Tigers of the 1990s are rapidly being eclipsed by their gigantic neighbor. Surely it is only a matter of time—10 years, 15 perhaps—until *chugoku shoku* ("China shock," as they say in Japan) is the most prominent feature of the global economic landscape.

Both nations and corporations must have a clear and robust strategy to both anticipate and respond to this new reality. Each must consider the potential impact of China's ascent. Will your company see China as a market opportunity, a competitive threat, a source of raw materials, a potential source of joint venture partnering, or a new manufacturing location? Are you ready to respond to these potential threats or opportunities? Have you considered these strategic questions:

- Is it likely that the relative importance of the Chinese market will change for your industry or value chain? What implications would this have for your strategic focus and product/market emphasis?
- Would doing business in China compromise your company's beliefs and values?
- What capabilities would be required to enter the Chinese marketplace?
- How might your competitors' decisions to move production facilities to China create a cost disadvantage for your firm?
- Will China do to you what Japan did to businesses in the late twentieth century? What lessons were learned then that apply now?

Whatever the answers for your organization, assumptions about the economic map of the twenty-first century will be heavily influenced by what happens in China.

THE MARKET OF ONE: UNLIMITED OPPORTUNITIES

Not every unknown is a problem. Companies must also think proactively about how they will exploit an unpredictable but foreseeable windfall.

One example: In 3 to 5 years, technology will have moved to a level of extraordinary personalization. Each of us will have a single handheld device, no larger than today's cellular telephones, with access to information, entertainment, communication, and commerce. After a long day at the office—or more likely not at the office—we'll use such a device to make a dinner reservation, get real-time verbal and visual directions via satellite tracking, sit down to our preordered favorite cocktails and fresh flowers, leave messages for our elderly parents and teenage children, and automatically debit our e-bank account when the bill is presented. In short, we will be connected to every aspect of business-to-business, business-to-consumer, and personal activity.

Such capabilities are not in the least farfetched. Their power can lead to the creation of a market of one, a possibility that entire industries (like document distribution) are well on their way to making a reality. Already, sophisticated monitoring of individual buying habits and consumer demographics is accomplished on a massive scale. Consumers may soon designate preferred vendors to respond to, or even anticipate, their needs for food, travel, entertainment, gifts, clothing, and so on based on a profile of individual preferences. Junk mail and 12-page advertising flyers will give way to targeted electronic communications—under the cover of a well-built firewall to protect privacy. Business-to-business marketing will surely be transformed by similar opportunities.

Internet commerce makes the concept of a supplier of one equally possible. Single Web sites offer replacement parts for every possible appliance manufacturer, and eBay alone offers a range of products beyond the wildest dreams of bricks-and-mortar warehousing.

The net effect of these shifts is to place enormous power in the hands of the individual consumer or corporate customer. Buyers are no longer passive recipients, and suppliers bypass traditional channels of distribution and industry limitations.

On the product side, organizations face a difficult paradox. The demand for highly customized product offerings—say, the implantable chip containing an individual's health history, medication program, and plan for preventive care—will take its place alongside the drive toward commoditization—perhaps an over-the-counter cure for the common cold. The demand for new products will create new forms of competition. For example, FDA approval of products based on traditional herbs and other easily obtained ingredients will raise the bar around the globe for pharmaceutical firms.

As part of your strategy reviews, questions like these should be raised:

- Do we understand how to balance the requirements of mass markets with the opportunities of the market of one and the capabilities needed?
- Are we confident that efforts to address markets of one will provide an appropriate return on our investments?
- What product development and market research would we need to do, and what information systems would we need to have, to identify, capture, and retain markets of one?

- How long will the market of one concept be around? Is it a fad?
- What are competitors doing to capitalize on these opportunities?

On the other hand, top teams will need to ensure they are not buying into certain fallacies:

- Doing more is not necessarily doing better. Any increase in the number of products and consumers will create additional complexity and may put the organization at risk for diluting its strategic intent.
- The unique competitive advantage of an organization does not automatically carry over into new product and market areas.
- Technology is an enabler, not a panacea. The potential return on opportunities must be balanced with an awareness of the capabilities and resources that will be required.

THE STRATEGIC LESSONS OF SEPTEMBER 11

I was on a plane the morning of September 11, flying from London to Chicago, and was subsequently stranded in Montreal for 3 days. There was a lot of time to try to absorb the horror of what had happened and its many implications.

The assumptions made by Western leaders about military and economic warfare have their roots in the campaigns of past military leaders: Alexander the Great, Napoleon, Wellington, and Patton. There were common elements in these conflicts; the enemy and its location were known or could be identified, the enemy's goals were clearly stated, its weapons were understood, and the rules of engagement for battle were generally agreed upon.

Not so the attacks of September 11. This "asymmetric warfare" was characterized by:

- An enemy that was initially unknown and hidden from view
- The element of surprise
- Its scale, audacity, and spectacular nature
- The willingness of the enemy to make sacrifices, even of their own lives
- The out-of-the-box thinking used to plan the attacks

- The lack of concern for the innocent and other "collateral" damage
- Near-flawless planning and execution
- New forms of weaponry (the aircraft themselves)
- Its intent to psychologically devastate and break morale
- The far-reaching economic, political, and social repercussions it created

This kind of combat has no pattern, balance, proportion, consistency, or coherence. It is entirely new and little understood. Similarly, responses to such an attack have been unlike any we have seen before. A vast array of overt and covert actions was launched on the military, diplomatic, political, financial, and psychological fronts. The military response alone encompassed conventional and guerilla warfare, special forces, assassination squads, and the overthrow of governments. The time frame of such efforts, as well as the rate of progress and the tactics required, is utterly different from traditional combat.

The extraordinary disruption of the rules of the game between people and nations that occurred on September 11 is the most dramatic sign of the uncertainty of our decade.

It will also be a source of insight for our boardrooms. Your assault on the marketplace and counterattacks from your competitors are now likely to incorporate "asymmetrical" characteristics. As you formulate and implement your strategy, you should be asking:

- How can we build an element of surprise into both our vision and its execution?
- What sacrifices are we prepared to make in order to achieve our goals?
- What opportunities are there for us to disrupt and destabilize our competition and the industry structure in order to gain advantage?
- How can we develop significantly different technological and product breakthroughs?
- Once we have made our moves, how can we make ourselves invulnerable to direct competitive attack?
- How audacious can we be in terms of new thinking, scale, and risk taking?

- How can we have an impact on all our competitors in a single strike?
- How can we win huge advantage with relatively little cost?
- How can we keep the competition guessing about our next moves?
- How can we lie low while planning our efforts in order to ensure the element of surprise?
- How can we implement our strategy speedily?

When your organization sets strategy, it must continually ask the unconventional questions if it is to stay in a competitive game characterized by asymmetric attacks.

There is another side of the coin here. Consider the actions of various governments and their agencies both before and after September 11:

- How well did international intelligence agencies gather, analyze, and share information and coordinate plans to act on that intelligence?
- Had any scenarios been developed that conceived of such an attack?
- If so, what plans were in place to prevent them?
- How were resources being allocated between conventional warfare and fighting international terrorism? Were investments made in new skills, new weaponry, different intellectual capital, and innovative logistics?
- How did the political, military, and intelligence communities plan to coordinate their efforts during such a crisis?

Lulled by a false sense of security, the U.S. government was clearly caught with its defenses down. Its leaders knew that an asymmetric assault could come any time, anywhere. But they did not act decisively. We hope that they and other governments around the world have learned that a large percentage of their resources must be devoted to identifying such potential problems and making concrete plans for dealing with them.

Even with the benefit of hindsight, the events of September 11 are difficult to understand. The next big attack, whether on the political or corporate front, is again likely to be asymmetrical in its scope, its surprise, and its potential devastation. The only chance of responding effectively will be based on a rigorous and creative approach to describing, preventing, and mitigating potential disasters.

Corporations, under threat of asymmetric assaults from competitors, will be challenged to do the same. Many must become asymmetric thinkers and players themselves. Creative thinking at the extremes of (legitimate) corporate behavior will serve them well in such an unpredictable world.

NO EASY ANSWERS

In times of discontinuity, an organization is always in danger of grasping at silver-bullet solutions. Alan Greenspan has described the lengthy stock market boom of the 1990s as a time of "irrational exuberance." In such a period, executives are tempted to believe they can defer strategic thinking indefinitely. But when a period of "irrational depression" follows, it is too late to shift gears.

During the past several years, no trend has been more compelling than the technology fix. But there is little difference between a technological miracle cure and other management fads executives turn to in the hot pursuit of excellence. Such initiatives must be adopted only if they are relevant and pursued within a robust strategic framework.

Most companies undertook a number of diverse initiatives in the last years of the twentieth century: enterprise resource planning, e-business, knowledge management, Six Sigma (again), the learning organization, business process re-engineering, and so on. They invested literally billions in such efforts. If your firm was among these, ask yourself: Was it worth it?

The next time a fad or the latest initiative comes your way, beware when you hear . . .

- "This is the answer."
- "If it's good enough for the best-performing companies, it's good enough for us."
- "This will help us expand our customer base"—or—"enable us to open up global markets"—or—"secure our positioning."
- "Our business processes are fine; we can handle this."

- "We'll just delegate implementation of this to functional specialists or an outside consultant."
- "We'll be up and running with this by the end of next quarter."
- "This is our number 1 priority."

Expect the range of management fads to grow in coming years—and avoid the pressure to jump on each new bandwagon to temper the effects of external change. Be cautious when snake-oil remedies are touted as a substitute for strategy—or threaten to dilute the focus on strategic objectives.

Top executives will do well to keep one eye on the latest management trends, and both hands firmly on the strategic tiller. The vision and its implementation are what will ultimately drive the organization's competitive power.

STRATEGY IN A CONTINGENT WORLD

Clear strategic thinking is not only possible in an age of discontinuity; it is an absolute requirement. Strategy is inherently flexible. It bears little resemblance to those long-range plans that were unwieldy exercises in corporate endurance: Change one number in the plan, and everything else had to change.

Strategy is about the top team's vision—and will. It is about forward thinking, rather than financial projections and trend lines into the unknown. It is about direction, not time. Strategy deals with what an organization *wants* to become.

In the last several years, the strategy process has evolved in response to change. We now challenge our clients to consider the "strategy beyond the strategy." We ask them to consider whether, as they continually review and update their current strategy, it will also provide a strong platform for what may follow.

Effective strategic thinking has become less linear than in more stable times. In particular, the constant examination of previously unheard of threats and opportunities—out-of-the-box thinking—has become increasingly important. The creativity applied in such thinking will be one of the most powerful weapons of an unpredictable, even arbitrary era.

What-If Thinking

The challenge is twofold—first, how to anticipate, and then how to respond, recover, and adapt.

To anticipate, top teams must be looking for thorough and creative answers to these questions:

- What could go wrong, and why?
- How can we prevent that? If our preventive actions fail, what contingency plans can we make to minimize the damage?
- What will be the impact on our strategy and its implementation? What modifications must we make?
- What opportunities might occur? What might go better than expected, and why?
- How could we make this happen and exploit such an opportunity?
- Is the exploitation of this opportunity aligned with our strategy? How will we test its viability in real-world practice? Again, how must we modify our strategy or its implementation?

We know of companies that excel at pushing their people to speculate, to dream, to imagine, to forecast, and to explore. Some forge alliances with world-renowned leaders on the technological front, like the MIT Media Lab. Top teams travel every year to sit at the feet of management guru Peter Drucker and learn from his futuristic insights. Prime Minister Tony Blair has established a "blue-sky unit" for the express purpose of thinking outside the box.

Such thinking must be woven through the entire strategy process. It begins when top teams create assumptions about social, political, economic, technological, and competitive trends and elicit the implications of those for their organization. The crafting of alternative visions allows the top team to frame possible responses to the what-if contingencies that could reshape an industry, yield a breakthrough technology or material, or ravage geographic markets.

Strategic Master Project Planning moves strategy from the boardroom to the marketplace; its implementation is in the hands of those closest to the action. And what-if thinking is the foundation for the iterative monitoring and reviewing of assumptions that keep strategic vision fresh and the organization nimble.

A robust, coherent strategy is the basis for making the difficult, fundamental choices that lie ahead. But a proven reliable process for dealing with "the slings and arrows of outrageous fortune" is just as important.

Response and Recovery

We're certain that even those companies most adversely affected by the events of September 11 are more likely to recover and move forward if they have been implementing, monitoring, and reviewing a clear strategy. They need to re-examine their strategic intelligence or bolster their approach to monitoring external trends. They need to take the Strategic Master Project Plan back to the drawing board and reallocate resources to 9/11 disaster recovery. But it is unlikely that their strategy as such will change.

The tools for adaptation and response must be built into the strategy process. An objective-driven approach to decision making, the analysis of potential problems and opportunities, and plans to meet them head on—these are powerful weapons in the twenty-first-century arena. They are backed by the strength of every component of the strategic profile. A company's Driving Force and competitive advantage, if established correctly in the first place, will remain sound. Implementation may be delayed, but strategy will remain the corporate anchor.

We live in remarkable times. For every unanticipated threat, there is an unforeseen opportunity. A disaster for one firm or industry often presents huge growth opportunities for others. Think of the worldwide boom in the security industry since September 11! The team that relentlessly pursues what-if thinking will be challenged, stretched, frustrated, yet ultimately rewarded. The team that remains focused on its central strategic precepts in the face of twenty-first-century mayhem will keep its vision viable and its organization ahead.

But every team needs a leader. While strategy permeates the organization at every level, it must also be driven from the top. In the final chapter, we examine the leadership characteristics required of every chief executive and those who will someday follow in his or her footsteps.

CHAPTER

14

Lessons for Strategic Leaders

The late Bob Morrison, once CEO of Consumers Packaging, used to say, "Managing the future of the organization is my unique responsibility. My power to influence what's currently going on in our organization is minimal, and that's not bad. Operational decisions have been made, and their implementation is already underway. My job is to focus relentlessly on our future. I must always think beyond what we are as an organization to envision what we should become."

Morrison was an exemplar in the art and discipline of strategic leadership. He ensured that there was no shortage of creative ideas and the means to implement them. He had the discipline to delegate implementation to those on the firing line. His experiences and those of the many other CEOs with whom we have worked illuminate a number of enduring lessons, not-so-obvious pitfalls, and practical guidelines for strategic leaders.

Leadership encompasses both art and discipline. It is certainly an art, since strategy formulation by definition deals with the unknowable future. Envisioning the future and painting pictures of your organization's response to it require great creativity. Even as you make the tough choices required to implement your vision and link strategy to operations, the art of creative thinking and developing new paradigms remains critical.

Discipline too is essential. A systematic thinking process moves a top team from formulating environmental assumptions and implications to selecting a Driving Force and developing the product/market matrix. During implementation, disciplined commitment is needed to keep everyone focused on strategic priorities in the face of competing—and legitimate—operational imperatives. And saying no to opportunities that are attractive but off strategy is tough. Again, discipline enables leaders to ensure that decisions made throughout the organization are consistent with strategy.

Strategic leadership draws deeply on the inner reserves of the CEO. Qualities such as decisiveness, drive, toughness, passion, integrity, a balance of optimism and realism, a willingness to delegate appropriately, and an ability to motivate the top team and every employee are prerequisites.

The notion of leadership has rightfully come under closer scrutiny in recent years. Chief executives are often encouraged to adopt one or another fashionable leadership model—the servant-leader, or the coach, or the team player—to unleash the potential of their people.

If only it were that simple. Every great chief executive we know has wrestled long and hard with two primary issues: how to set and implement strategy, and how to develop, motivate, and unite the top team in their commitment to it. *The most successful leaders—those who have been able to craft their strategic visions and bring them to life—take personal responsibility for strategy.* They also know it cannot be done alone.

The reins of top management responsibility must continuously be passed on to future generations of strategic leaders. The young tigers in our companies risk being seduced by the proliferation of specialized knowledge, the attraction of technological solutions, and the mandate for speedy action arising from external change. Firm and reliable anchors are few and far between. Perhaps the biggest challenge for the new breed of leaders will be to avoid the trap of diluting the requirement for focus.

Process is an anchor in setting and implementing strategy. No matter how tough the tasks of strategy may be, it is systematic process that enables senior teams to think clearly and incisively about strategy and achieve breakthroughs for the future.

What makes process so powerful? The answer is as old as the Socratic dialogue. It is the strength of disciplined, systematic questioning. This discipline cuts through the clutter and complexity to organize data, test answers, and make reasoned judgments.

Many other lessons we have learned are worth remembering. Just as a clear strategy shows what to do, as well as what *not* to do, so leaders should note both the pitfalls to avoid as well as best practice from which to learn.

The most seductive pitfalls are these:

- Losing focus
- Shortchanging the time devoted to quality thinking
- Being distracted by both operational and financial minutiae
- Lacking a clear and robust process for setting and implementing strategy
- Allowing a weak leadership team to perpetuate the status quo
- Avoiding legitimate, strong challenges from others
- Insisting on micromanaging the details of implementation
- Being averse to taking strategic risks for fear of failure
- Failing to develop the strategic capabilities of key managers and executives
- Taking for granted the collective and committed ownership of a vision, and leaving to chance the actions needed from every stakeholder to implement it
- Being inconsistent and paying lip service only to the strategy and its implementation, without behaving as others are expected to do (do as I say, not as I do)
- Ducking the role of prime motivator
- Delegating the responsibility for setting strategy to management consultants

On the other hand, best-practice strategic leadership is achieved when CEOs:

- Model, stimulate, foster, support, and reward strategic thinking
- Prepare high-potential executives for their strategic leadership roles before they reach the top
- Own the integrity of the entire strategic process: not just the intellectual stimulation and glamour in formulation but also the

genius required for implementation and the toughness of charac-
ter needed to keep strategy monitored, reviewed, and updated
- Make the tough choices
- Communicate early and often. Be honest and clear; avoid ambi-
guity and dissembling
- Serve as a cultural role model
- Create and sustain a performance system that ensures recogni-
tion and reward for strategic performance
- Take charge. When the going gets tough, the tough get going.
Do not be dissuaded. Stand fast and demonstrate courage

Great leaders are judged as much by what they leave behind as by
what they achieve during their tenure. A vibrant, vital organization that
is fiercely competitive and driven to excel is, of course, an important
legacy for any leader. This means having in place a high-performing
leadership team, a thinking organization, and managers and employees
at all levels passionately committed to getting things done.

But a CEO is the ultimate custodian of strategic well-being. The
most enduring contribution to the organization and its stakeholders—
and the hallmark of a great leader—is the legacy of a clear, exciting, and
robust strategy, paired with a deep reservoir of talent ready to assume
the responsibilities for the art and discipline of strategic leadership.

Endnotes

Chapter 2

1. Alan Brache, *How Organizations Work: Taking a Holistic Approach to Enterprise Health* (New York: John Wiley & Sons, 2002).
2. This breakthrough thinking on the matrix relationship between strategy and operations first appeared in *Top Management Strategy: What It Is and How to Make It Work*, by Benjamin B. Tregoe and John W. Zimmerman (New York: Simon & Schuster, 1981) as shown here:

3. For a fuller consideration of rational process, see *The New Rational Manager*, by Charles H. Kepner and Benjamin B. Tregoe (Princeton, N.J.: Princeton Research Press, 1981).

Chapter 5

1. Benjamin B. Tregoe and John W. Zimmerman, *Top Management Strategy: What It Is and How to Make It Work* (New York: Simon & Schuster, 1981).
2. Robert A. Lutz, *Guts: The Seven Laws of Business That Made Chrysler the World's Hottest Car Company* (New York: John Wiley & Sons, 1998).
3. Tregoe and Zimmerman, *Top Management Strategy*.
4. For a more detailed discussion of decision analysis, see Charles H. Kepner and Benjamin B. Tregoe, *The New Rational Manager* (Princeton, N.J.: Princeton Research Press, 1981).

Chapter 9

1. Alan Brache, *How Organizations Work: Taking a Holistic Approach to Enterprise Health* (New York: John Wiley & Sons, 2002).

Chapter 10

1. Mike Freedman, "Viewpoint: Creating a Strategic Culture," *Strategic Direction* 16, no. 2 (February 2000): 3–4.
2. The performance system model was first published in 1984, copyright Kepner-Tregoe, Inc. "Managing Performance Is More than Managing People," *Business*, Volume VII, no. 1 (April-May-June 1984): 46–48.

Chapter 11

1. Robert Heller, "How BA Engineered its Turnaround," *Management Today* (September 1992): 50–55.

Index

Thinking, strategic (*see* Strategic
  thinking)
3G technology, 1, 40, 108
Time frame, strategic, 8, 45–47
Time management, 152
Todd, Doug, 24, 126–127, 153
Top management/top team:
  commitment of, 10, 21, 23, 106, 179
  communication role of, 165–170
  decision-making role of, 180–181
  rules for, 38–39
  structure of, 129–131
Towngas (*see* Hong Kong and China
  Gas Company Limited)
Toys R Us, 59
Trends, 31, 190
Trust House Forte, 173
TRW, 72
Tungsten, 34, 108
Tyco, 9, 63
Type of emphasis, 95

U
United Kingdom, 4–6
Universality (of basic beliefs), 52
Upstream, 12
U.S. Forest Service, 83–84

V
Value chains, 12, 32–33
Varity Corporation, 71–72, 85
Viability, 185
Vietnam, 190
Vision, 9, 65
Vivendi, 189
Vodaphone, 1
Vulnerability, strategic, 2, 10

W
Walkman, 97
Wall Street (film), 9
Wall Street Journal, 162
Warfare, asymmetric, 193–196
Warren, Jeff, 138–139, 173
Welch, Jack, 154
Wellington, Duke of, 193
What-if thinking, 73–75,
  198–199
World-class companies, 188
World Trade Organization, 48
WorldCom, 9
Writers, 73

X
Xerox, 8, 9, 46, 84, 161–162

ABOUT THE AUTHORS

Mike Freedman is president of the Worldwide Strategy Practice of Kepner-Tregoe, Inc., the global consulting and training company with corporate headquarters in Princeton, New Jersey. During 20 years with the firm, he has led many consulting assignments designed to facilitate clients in the formulation and implementation of their strategies. These assignments have led him all over the globe and into Fortune 500 and FTSE 100 companies, governments, public-sector industries, private firms and not-for-profit institutions. His clients have included the American Manufacturing Corporation, the Bank of Ireland, Bristol and West Bank, Corning, Courtaulds, Chase Manhattan Bank NV, Hallmark, the Industrial Development Agency of Ireland, ICI Paints, Kennametal Inc., Lagoven (the state oil company of Venezuela), Massey-Ferguson, Royal Mail, and the Savoy Group of Hotels.

Mr. Freedman has lived and worked in the United Kingdom, Canada, the United States, Iran, and Singapore. It is against this rich background and his more than 15 years as a senior executive in Xerox, Hertz Rent A Car, and Philips that this book has been written. He has also been active in political and community affairs. Mr. Freedman served as personal advisor to Tom (now Lord) Sawyer when the latter was general secretary of the Labour Party in the 3-year run up to Tony Blair's success in the 1997 general election. He also stood for Parliament in earlier general elections in the United Kingdom.

Mr. Freedman is a former president of the U.K. Management Consultancies Association, which is the professional and trade body of major consulting firms. He has published more than a dozen articles on strategy, and he is on the editorial board of the United Kingdom–based journal *Strategic Direction*. He studied as an undergraduate at University College, London, and as a postgraduate at the Universities of Oxford and Saskatchewan in Canada. He has been a non-executive director of a financial services firm and is currently on the boards of Revise.It, an Internet-based student portal, and SAS, a corporate design and communications agency.

Mike and his wife, Avril, a physician, have five grown children.

Benjamin B. Tregoe is cofounder and chairman emeritus of Kepner-Tregoe, Inc. He also serves as chairman of the Tregoe Education Forum, a nonprofit foundation established in 1993 to support public education reform.

Kepner-Tregoe was founded in 1958 on the strength of pioneering research conducted by Dr. Tregoe and Dr. Charles H. Kepner on rational problem solving and decision making. Since then, the Kepner-Tregoe approach has been transferred to more than 10 million managers and workers in thousands of companies around the world.

With John W. Zimmerman, Dr. Tregoe also developed a groundbreaking process for strategic decision making. This process has since been applied by hundreds of organizations to setting and implementing strategy, and Dr. Tregoe has consulted with top management teams to help formulate the strategic direction of a large number of companies in North America, Asia, and Europe.

Dr. Tregoe is a sought-after lecturer and has published extensively. In 1965 he and Dr. Kepner coauthored *The Rational Manager*, a landmark book in management methodology. He has coauthored other management texts including *Top Management Strategy: What It Is and How to Make It Work* (1980), *Vision in Action: Putting a Winning Strategy to Work* (1989), and *The Culture of Success* (with Mr. Zimmerman, 1997).

Dr. Tregoe graduated from Whittier College and earned his Ph.D. from Harvard. He was awarded an honorary LL.D. from Whittier College, where he served as a trustee. He has also served on the boards of the J.M. Smucker Company, the World Affairs Council of Philadelphia, and the National Alliance of Business, and chaired the Advisory Committee to the Dean of the Graduate School of Arts and Sciences of Harvard University. Dr. Tregoe is a member of the Human Resources Development Hall of Fame.